DATE DUE

GAYLORD		PRINTED IN U.S.A.

* THE *
# ANATOMY
OF ISRAEL'S
SURVIVAL

· THE ·
ANATOMY
OF ISRAEL'S
SURVIVAL
· · · · · ·
HIRSH
GOODMAN

PublicAffairs
New York

Published in the United States by PublicAffairs™,
a Member of the Perseus Books Group

PublicAffairs books are available at special discounts for bulk purchases in the U.S. by corporations, institutions, and other organizations. For more information, please contact the Special Markets Department at the Perseus Books Group, 2300 Chestnut Street, Suite 200, Philadelphia, PA 19103, call (800) 810-4145, ext. 5000, or e-mail special.markets@perseusbooks.com.

Book Design by Pauline Brown
Typeset in 12 point Goudy Oldstyle Std by the Perseus Books Group

Library of Congress Cataloging-in-Publication Data

Goodman, Hirsh.
    The anatomy of Israel's survival / Hirsh Goodman.—1st ed.
        p.   cm.
    Includes index.
    ISBN 978-1-58648-529-0 (hardcover)—ISBN 978-1-61039-083-5 (electronic)
1. Arab-Israeli conflict. 2. Arab-Israeli conflict—1993——Peace. 3. Israel—Poliics and government—1993– 4. Palestinian Arabs—Politics and government. 5. Diplomatic negotiations in international disputes. I. Title.
DS119.7.G6439 2011
956.9405'4—dc23
                                                              2011023352

First Edition

10 9 8 7 6 5 4 3 2 1

*For Lev, Gavriel, Maya, and Shai, in the hope that
they may know peace in their time, and especially
for Isabel, my friend and counsel.*

CONTENTS

CONTENTS

PROLOGUE

Can Israel survive? The question used to infuriate me. Does someone wake up in Britain, or America, or even Burundi, and ask themselves whether their country can survive? Wasn't it just bizarre that after over sixty years as an independent state, there were still those who questioned Israel's longevity and, by implication, its legitimacy?

It has taken me years to understand there is much merit to the question, for both Israel and its enemies.

Modern Israel faces challenges from Arab demography; the explosion of the ultraorthodox community; enemies to the north, east, and south, and as far away as Iran; and terrorism from closer to home. It is a young country with young institutions. Its liberal and independent legal system is under constant attack from the right wing and Orthodox, and its democracy both entrenched and fragile at the same time. It has no natural resources to speak of other than brainpower, and this, too, is subject to instability given the lure of globalization.

As things are now, Israel stands to do itself more damage through peace than in any war. If a peace is agreed on that requires massive population transfers, the resultant internal dissension could be potentially more damaging to Israel than external conflict. Thus, in war and in peace, Israel is threatened.

In May 2011, U.S. President Barak Obama called for negotiations for a Palestinian state based on the 1967 lines with appropriate land swaps. Israel's prime minister, Binyamin Netanyahu, responded by saying Israel could never return to the 1967 boundaries, which he called "indefensible." Israel and its most important ally, the United States, seemed to be on a collision course.

Now, with over one hundred countries demanding that a Palestinian state be established within the 1967 borders, even unilaterally, and the Middle East exploding around it unpredictably, the pressures on Israel seem greater than ever before.

All this is only the tip of the iceberg.

ONE

The Cutting Edge

Of all the existential threats Israel faces, other than civil war, common wisdom has it that Iran is at the top of the list. Iran is maniacally dedicated to Israel's destruction, and says so on every occasion, in every language, and at every opportunity. By now even the parrots in the Teheran zoo can repeat the mantras of hatred calling for Israel to be wiped off the map, its people sent back to Poland, Palestine liberated, for the cancer to be removed from Arabia, and the West's agent of evil, Israel, crushed and expelled.

Not since Hitler have the Jewish people theoretically faced such a threat. Half of the world's Jewish population currently lives in Israel. Now, like then, the Jews actually have very little to do with the problem, but provide a convenient whipping boy for the Iranian regime and its aspirations of regional hegemony and control of the Gulf. Israel has no unavoidable disputes with Iran once you get past its right to exist—no common borders or contested resources. The two countries' armies have never clashed. Yet it is ostensibly because of Israel that Iran is rushing to attain nuclear weapons and expending considerable amounts on missile and satellite programs, among the other weapons it is amassing for its day in the field with the Jewish state. Or so Teheran says.

A nuclear Iran, it is now recognized, is not Israel's problem alone. It possesses missiles that bring the Gulf states, Egypt, Turkey, Europe, and Russia all within reach. A nuclear Iran would be transformative, a country not easily gone to war against, and one that will have considerably more power on the regional stage. And if Iran goes nuclear, it is almost certain that Turkey and Egypt will accelerate their own programs and Saudi Arabia would buy an off-the-shelf bomb from Pakistan. Libya agreed to dismantle its nuclear program in December 2003. The international crisis that broke out with Colonel Qaddafi's regime in March 2011 would have looked very different had Qaddafi had the bomb.

A nuclear Middle East is in no one's interest; therefore, opposition to the prospect is wide. The United States, China, and Russia have imposed sanctions on Iran in the hope of impeding the bomb. Israel and Saudi Arabia find themselves on the same side of the fence.

But Iran is Israel's problem most of all. No other country is existentially threatened by Iran, in a position to suffer irreparable damage if attacked with nuclear weapons. Those imposing sanctions and locked in diplomacy to try to resolve the problem are involved in global power play, not a life-and-death situation. Iran is not calling for the destruction of Turkey or Saudi Arabia, and if America, China, or Russia loses the game, as they indeed might, it is not their heads that will be on the chopping block.

For Israel, there is no margin for error. Over 70 percent of Israel's population, one-third of all the Jews in the world, and its ports, airports, refining capacities, and industry are located along the coastal plain, 161 miles long from north to south and some ten miles deep, about the size of an average game park in Africa. I took a helicopter ride recently, taking off from the Herzliah airfield just north of Tel Aviv. Hardly six hundred feet in the air and you see it all in the palm of your hand, from Ashkelon shimmering in the south to the Haifa bay and Acre in the north, the cities of Holon, Rehovot, Nes Tsiona, Petah Tikva, Netanya, Ramat Gan, Kfar Saba, all packed together like eggs in one basket. Along the coast are the chimneys of power stations and desalination plants, ports and tourist areas. The highways to either side are packed with afternoon traffic and the new office and residential towers that have sprouted up between Tel Aviv and Ramat Gan, glowing in the sunset. In one glance you can see five of the country's major universities, all of its ports, its major international airport, highways, railways, and the center of its business life. I remember the pictures from Hiroshima and Nagasaki and think of what happened there. Imagine the devastation of a bomb five, ten, a hundred times more powerful in an area as dense as this one, humming with traffic and life underneath. If attacked with nuclear weapons it would be, to use a phrase attributed to Moshe Dayan, "the destruction of the Third Temple." Everything would be lost. There would be no second chance.

The Iranians know this; hence the temptation, the dream, that it could be done, even knowing that Iran would suffer terribly as a result. But with a population ten times that of Israel and a country seventy-five times as large, Iran reckons that no matter how harsh the punishment meted out in return for attacking Israel, it would be mauled, not killed. In this context, none of the symmetry and deterrence that kept the Cold War cold applies, and there is none of the diplomatic pragmatism that even the most repressive Soviet leaders possessed. Iran's regime is based on brute power; its calculations cannot be put into a rational context. From Israel's point of view, they must be taken at their word. To do otherwise would be to invite catastrophe.

Yet of all Israel's major problems, the Iran one is "simplest" to deal with. It carries none of the contention of a potential settlement with the Palestinians, or even with the Syrians if Israel has to give up the Golan Heights in return for peace. There is no internal debate in Israel as to how to approach the Iranian issue, or whether too much money is spent on countering it. It is not an electoral issue, and it crosses all political boundaries. No pro-Iran lobbyists are to be found in the Knesset, even among the most vocal Arab opponents of the Zionist Jewish state.

What the Iranians may not know and appreciate is that, in a very strange way, Israel actually owes them a debt of gratitude. Their threats and capabilities have forced Israel to focus its mind like never before, with an end result that keeps Israel at the cutting edge of technology, and its economy vibrant and productive, though poor in natural resources and even water.

Israel has deep respect for the Iranians. It has watched with awe as the regime has sent thousands of graduates through universities in the West, many returning to work in the Iranian military industries. Israelis have seen the Iranians dance around UN bureaucrats in Vienna and other locations, attempting to slow down their march toward nuclear independence through an inspection regime that was almost laughable. They have defied the "great powers" and thumbed their nose at successive American administrations, weaving and dodging and playing one side against the other. Though regressed, they have overcome attempts by the Mossad, CIA, and others to quietly sabotage their program, and have taken great care to make their assembly lines as protected as possible. Even after the supposedly devastating STUXNET computer virus attack that hit its enrichment plants, Iran managed to keep 5,200 of its 8,000 centrifuges spinning and producing fissile materials.

The regime has managed to buy materials and components for bomb-making from an astounding array of suppliers, often without the seller knowing, or caring, who the end party was. They have done this through a network of companies that make a spider's web look uncomplicated. They move their secret headquarters around often to avoid detection by Western intelligence agencies, like in 2008 when the nuclear research center in central Teheran was leveled to become a public park, leading the CIA to announce that year that the Iranians had closed down their military nuclear program, and Israeli intelligence chiefs to pull out their hair in frustration, knowing that it had been reopened across town. "Don't they understand that while buildings can be destroyed, all they have to do is move the brains down the road in a bus and open up again?" said then Israeli intelligence chief Amos Yadlin at a meeting on the subject one afternoon.

There is also no question that the Iranians have parallel programs in operation. The world's attention was, and is, focused on

Bushehr, but in September 2009, a second nuclear facility was revealed to the world by Israeli intelligence, the evidence reportedly being brought to Washington and Russia personally by the prime minister, Binyamin Netanyahu, which showed the enrichment plant deep in the mountains at Fordo, just twenty kilometers from the holy city of Qom, with the capacity to produce one bomb a year and growing.

"Have respect for your enemy" is one of the oldest maxims in the Israeli army, and Israel knows the Iranians well. Tens of thousands of Jews left Iran and now live in Israel, and, until the 1979 revolution that saw the demise of the shah and his repressive regime, and the takeover by the ayatollahs and an even more repressive regime, Israel and Iran had close ties. The shah provided Israel with oil, and Israel provided him with military assistance that included conventional weapons, as well as intercontinental ballistic missiles, code-named "Jericho," and perhaps advice on how to develop Iran's nuclear program, started under the American "Atoms for Peace" initiative in the 1950s, into something more "meaningful."

Mahmoud Ahmadinejad, the Iranian president, is often portrayed in the Western media as an almost ludicrous figure, with his histrionic rants against Israel and risible efforts to prove the Holocaust never happened. But he is no fool. On his watch he has moved over Iran's core assets to the control of the Revolutionary Guards, fervently loyal to the regime, including state-owned industries, key security units, and elements of the Iranian armed forces, like the nuclear program and the missile forces, which do not fall under the purview of the chief of staff. The Guards also control the anti-aircraft units in case air force officers, considered generally more secular and educated and thus less trustworthy, were to decide to stage a coup. Ahmadinejad has managed to contain bread and fuel riots, and cut subsidies, something previously thought politically impossible, and steal an election in 2009, when his opposition disappeared into dark dungeons as the results came in.

Iran spends only 2.5 percent of its GDP on the military, yet it has managed to move into the space age with satellites and provide its military with an impressive arsenal of advanced ballistic missiles and sophisticated command and control systems, and its people with Soviet-style military parades from time to time, often accompanied by endless television footage of visits to the country's nuclear facilities and the smoke trails of missiles as they streak off into the air.

This is a sinister regime that works in sinister ways. It uses terror, surrogates, and subterfuge with impunity around the world. It took twelve years but in 2006 it was conclusively proved that Iran was responsible for the attack on the Jewish community center in Buenos Aires on July 18, 1994. In this, Argentina's most deadly bombing, eighty-seven people died and over one hundred people were injured, many of them passersby. The Islamic Jihad took responsibility, as it did for the March 1992 bombing in the same city that left twenty-nine dead, many of them children at a school in a nearby church. The truth was known well in advance of 2006, but obfuscated by investigators of questionable reliability, some reportedly paid off by the Argentinean government itself, then deep in nuclear collusion with the Iranians.

Since then, however, Iran has developed ever more subterfuge. It has created entire legions abroad, openly identified with the regime in Teheran and totally committed to doing its bidding. Hezbollah in Lebanon is one such example. Iran very neatly stepped into the vacuum created by the 1982 Israeli invasion of Lebanon. Teheran sent in a contingent from the Revolutionary Guards who with skill and dedication managed to train, fund, arm, and bring together a political party, Hezbollah, the Party of God. Within a decade, Hezbollah's own private army would become the most powerful force in a country once known as the Switzerland of the Middle East, where Saudi princes came to gamble and whisper French into the ears of professional ladies, and eat from forbidden fruits.

After years of tensions, cat-and-mouse games, and mud-hurling at each other, in 2006 Hezbollah provoked a war with Israel, both sides eventually coming off somewhat mauled: Hezbollah, and parts of Lebanon with it, were pounded into the ground, the south of the country left deserted, Lebanon's oil and other infrastructure destroyed, and Hezbollah's stronghold in the Dahieh quarter of Beirut reduced to rubble in which over 1,000 people were killed. The Israelis suffered many fewer casualties and physical damage, but the psychological damage was immense. Suddenly the whole country became a battlefield as rockets fell freely on major cities like Haifa and close to the country's main petrochemical refineries in the Acre bay area. No longer was war a distant reality: Israel's cities were now exposed to the whims of paramilitary forces controlled by an enemy thousands of kilometers away.

Since 2006, with Syrian help, Hezbollah has gotten back on its feet. It has two wings—civilian and military—and wields much power in Lebanese politics through its parliamentary delegation, and in the field with its force of 15,000 men under arms and an arsenal of 45,000 rockets able to reach deep into Israel, presumably in part to deter Israel from attacking Iran's nuclear facilities. In January 2011 Hezbollah showed the full extent of its power when it ousted the government of Saad Hariri and installed Najia Mikati, a pro-Syria billionaire, in his place. Hariri had threatened to go ahead and cooperate with a UN investigation into the 2005 assassination of his father, Rafik, the findings of which would have implicated both Syria and Hezbollah. Both Hariris had been popular with the people and tolerated by Hezbollah as long as they toed the line. The minute the Iran-backed militia wanted them out, however, they found themselves on the street with much sympathy from the world but powerless to wrest the fate of Lebanon from the hands of Hezbollah and its Iranian minders.

Lebanon is not the only country to feel the reach of Iran's long arm. It is involved in Afghanistan, where its diplomats have been documented handing over wads of cash to the Karzai government through Umar Daudzai, the president's most loyal aide, in the hope of driving a wedge between the Afghan government and its American supporters. In March 2011 British special forces in Afghanistan intercepted a convoy of three trucks, deep in the Nimruz province, which contained forty-eight 122mm rockets destined for the Taliban. This was the latest of over sixty such interceptions in three years, ranging from ammunition and small arms to mortars and rockets. And Iran's involvement in Iraq is deep and consequential. In 2010, Iranian weapons and instructors of how to use these weapons were discovered hard at work in Africa. Major Iranian arms shipments were intercepted on their way to rebels in Nigeria, Gambia, and Senegal. But in Gaza, its takeover through Hamas, and specifically the Palestinian Islamic

Jihad, which reports directly to the Iranian secret service, has been total, creating an entire country, a mini-Iran, on Israel's southern border, an ideal base from which to shell not only Israeli settlements to the east and north but also Israel's nuclear facility in Dimona, the symbol of Israeli survival and resistance, its doomsday weapon.

Though Gaza's mostly Palestinian refugee population is Sunni, this has not stopped the Shia Iranians from striking a bond between them, using a system of orphanages, soup kitchens, free kindergartens, schools, universities, and mosques to solidify Hamas's control of the Strip. With its population of 1.5 million and growing fast, and strategically placed on Israel's border, Gaza is an excellent base of operation for the Iranians. So deep is Iranian involvement in Gaza that Iranian intelligence has set up its own units, the Palestinian Islamic Jihad, in the Strip who act independently of Hamas when Iran's agenda and that of the Palestinians part ways. In March 2011, for example, when Hamas and the Palestinian Authority on the West Bank began to think of reconciliation talks, the Palestinian Islamic Jihad launched dozens of mortars against empty fields in Israel to escalate the situation and send a clear message that from the Islamic Jihad's point of view, conciliation between the warring Palestinian factions was not on the agenda at that time.

Since June 2007, when Hamas took over Gaza, Israel has had Iranian divisions on its northern and southern borders. The soldiers themselves may not be Iranian, though Iranian advisers were always there to help. Still, many of the men and all the senior commanders of these units have been trained in Iran, and recruits who are seen to have a future attend an Iranian surrogate boot camp just west of Teheran that is shaped like a round cake: one segment Hezbollah, another Hamas, then Islamic Jihad, Taliban, and others as per need. Each group is trained separately to deal with the specific enemy and mission they face, but they are also brought together to exchange information and views. They undergo conventional weapon and sabotage training, but importantly are brought into the cyber age, given codes and intelligence methods to maintain secret lines of communication with Iran.

In this way, although there is no rational strategic reason for a quarrel between Israel and Iran, Israel now faces potential nuclear destruction in the worst case, or multiple missile attacks from Iran, Lebanon, and Gaza in a time of war, threatening all of Israel's cities, infrastructure, and defense. The nuclear threat aside, its implementation being immensely complicated and highly unlikely, the presence of quasi-Iranian forces on two of Israel's borders carries with it a host of tactical advantages for the Iranians, and serious disadvantages for Israel. Hezbollah and Hamas are there as troublemakers and to keep Israel's eye off the ball: Iran itself. They can be used to escalate the situation when needed, even to the point of all-out conflict and international crisis—as in 2006 and the Gaza campaign in 2008—to force Israel to dedicate massive expenditures to fortify its northern and southern borders, and to find expensive solutions to stop primitive rockets from paralyzing entire cities. For example, the Iron Dome anti-rocket system Israel deployed in March 2011 as a shield against incoming rockets from Gaza cost $250 million to develop and costs $40,000 each time it is used. A local joke is that if the Palestinians wanted to break Israel's economy, all they had to do is fire several hundred rockets a day toward one of the country's southern cities for several years. The Iron Dome, however, is built to discern which rockets are on a trajectory to cause damage and which are not, limiting this possibility. Despite massive initial skepticism about the Iron Dome's true capabilities and its cost, in its first baptism of fire over the weekend of April 8–9, 2011, it downed eight out of nine rockets heading for Beersheba and Ashkelon, Israel's two major southern cities. The ninth landed in an empty field, causing no damage. This success damped criticism but did not obviate the truth that the deployment of Iran-controlled rockets on Israel's southern border is another factor that diverts Israeli strategic resources from pursuing the real objective: thwarting a nuclear Iran.

Also, with Israeli intelligence busy with Hezbollah and Hamas, it has fewer resources to focus on Iran itself. There is a limit to how much the intelligence arm of a small country like Israel can deal with, how many spies it can field at any one time. Because of the way Hezbollah and Hamas fight, hidden deep among civilians in densely populated cities, every time Israel responds to an attack, there is an international outcry. Commissions of inquiry are set up in the UN and another nail is hammered into the coffin of Israel's public diplomacy. Be it through Holocaust denial or international condemnation, Israel's continued de-legitimization is a peg of Iranian foreign policy, and what better tool than flooding the airwaves with pictures of Jews killing innocent Arab women and children in response to attacks from Gaza and Lebanon? The Iranians have come to understand full well that the world's memory is as long as the last newscast.

The damage to Israel from border wars is tremendous. Already the country spends 9 percent of its GDP on defense, the highest ratio in the developed world. In 2010 defense expenditure reached a record high of 16 percent of the overall budget, just under $15 billion, and that was just for the military. The Atomic Energy Commission, the Mossad, and the secret service are accounted for out of the prime minister's office, and the police have their own ministry and budget line. On the military Israel spends around $2,300 per person per year, exclusive of the prime minister's office. If you add the home guard, emergency services, public bomb shelters, border police, compulsory bombproof rooms built in every house, and every citizen, from babies up, provided with personal gas masks, Israel probably spends more per person on security than the annual earnings of most of the world's population.

Now add to this the cost of the last war in Lebanon, for example, and defense outlays become atmospheric, stretching to the core the money available for research budgets and dealing with Iran. According to official Israeli figures, the 2006 conflict with Hezbollah cost the lives of 119 soldiers and 43 civilians, including 18 Arabs. Hundreds more were seriously wounded. The direct cost to the economy was $1.6 billion, or 1.5 percent of GDP. The total cost of carrying out the war was $5.5 billion. For over a month, from July 12 to August 14, some 630 factories were closed and 300,000 people displaced. At various times one million people lived in bomb shelters, 6,000 homes were hit by rockets, and the damage to some of Israel's most beautiful forests will take more than forty years to repair. The direct cost to Iran? Zero, other than the expense of replacing Hezbollah's arsenals with newer and more sophisticated weapons for the next round. Lebanon paid a heavy price with 1,300 dead, mainly civilians, and its airport, oil infrastructure, and roads, particularly in the south, badly damaged. But Lebanon's pain is not felt in Teheran.

As in every war there were serious conclusions to be drawn from the Lebanese conflict touched off by Hezbollah's kidnapping and killing of soldiers in a cross-border raid. For Israel they mainly pertained to the failure of the ground forces, leading to one of the most serious shake-ups in the army since the 1973 Yom Kippur War. Heads rolled, commissions of inquiry were established, and lessons were learned. Hezbollah learned that in the future it had better tread lightly with Israel. It did not expect the punishing harshness of Israel's response and to this day its leadership is careful when coming out of their underground bunkers. Israel was humbled when a supermodern, superexpensive Sa'ar Five-class missile boat, the Corvette INS *Hanit*, was taken out on the second evening of the war off the coast of Tyre—at the time the crew was welcoming the Sabbath and left their early-warning devices off—by an Iranian-supplied C-802 antiship missile fired from the coast. But from then on for Hezbollah it was mostly downhill.

In the ground conflict against Hezbollah, Israeli forces prevailed, but many failings were discovered in their operational capabilities, especially among reserve forces, which make up 80 percent of the military. The truth of the matter, however, was that the neglect in the ground forces was almost by design. The defense budget had been stretched by the Second Intifada and by trying to counter the Iranian threat. The chances of a ground war were considered negligible since Iraq, once Israel's deadliest enemy on its eastern front, had been destroyed in two American-led wars; there was peace with Jordan and Egypt; Lebanon had no army to speak of; and Syria had not invested in ground units for years, concentrating instead on rockets and missiles. Though Hezbollah was seen as a threat, it was not considered capable of fielding a conventional enemy army. It was a serious irritant that would be dealt with from the air and by other means. It did not have tanks or armored personnel carriers, but was built on stealth, rockets, and infrastructure placed deep in the hearts of civilian populations.

But while Israel's performance on the ground left a lot to be desired, there was one aspect of the Israeli military's performance Hezbollah, the Iranians, and others must have noticed: the total destruction of fifty-nine long- and medium-range missile launchers supplied by Iran and Syria that Hezbollah had stockpiled and prepared for use. These were destroyed in thirty-nine minutes in a stunning air campaign indicative of just how advanced Israeli's ability to deal with sophisticated threats had become.

To do this was infinitely more complicated than Israel's surprise attack on the Arab airfields in 1967, before the birth of the first computer in military service. It required the orchestration of aircraft, drones, airborne command and control systems, satellites, precise and sophisticated deep-penetrating bombs, and more than anything else intelligence, which, judging from the results, was obviously brilliant.

What they saw in Lebanon was highly indicative of a supersmart military that had managed to integrate cutting-edge technologies into a powerful fighting force. For those who analyze warfare, and surely the Iranians do, the destruction of the missiles in so short a time was a sobering lesson. The air force cannot deal effectively with individually fired sixty-year-old Katyusha rockets being dumped over the border, causing relatively little damage, but give them an electronic, radar, or heat signature, and *boom!*—the threat is gone. The more sophisticated warfare becomes, the greater Israel's advantage. The more technology dependent Hezbollah becomes, the easier a target it becomes. That is Israel's cutting edge, the cornerstone of its defense policy, and the war in 2006 was but one tiny glimpse into it.

Israel's greatest asset is its ingenuity. This by definition means a lack of discipline, behaving and thinking outside the box. To focus its mind, Israel needs a national project. In the 1980s it was the Lavi fighter jet, a beautiful aircraft designed by pilots for pilots with groundbreaking technology in avionics, electronics, and aerodynamic design. The project was canceled in 1987 under pressure from the American government, which preferred that Israel spend its American aid dollars on American-made F-16s, not on an independent project in Israel.

The Lavi brought together some of the finest engineering minds in the country. They worked on information management systems, radars, communications, navigation, avionics, electronics, fly-by-wire systems, miniaturization, optics, metals, carbon compounds, and aeronautics. When the project was canceled after hundreds of millions of dollars in investment, some 1,500 highly trained scientists and engineers were released into the economy and became the basis for Israel's high-tech industry. Iran has taken over where the Lavi left off. Countering its threat is Israel's new national project, keeping its only national resource, brainpower, working away at top speed. Obviously the world would be a better place with a democratic Iran and for Israel that would be a double blessing, the removal of a threat and the renewing of historic ties. But in the meantime Iran should know that to a large degree it is the engine of Israeli industrial and scientific growth, having made it essential for the country to seek out its most promising young minds in the school system at a fairly young age and move these teenagers into a specialized education enrichment program. They go into the army at eighteen, receive bachelor's degrees at nineteen and their second degrees at twenty-three, and are released back into the workforce at the age of twenty-six, often holding higher degrees from Israel's premier educational institutions. While in service they break codes, sift through intelligence, apply sciences, and grapple with problems posed by a smart, sinister, and potentially dangerous enemy thousands of miles away. Then they come into the workforce. My good friend Doron Susslik, a veteran senior employee of Israel Aircraft Industries, the country's major defense and civilian concern, has shown nothing but patience with me. For many months he opened door after door to me. It was stunning to see Israel's capacity, from a nano-drone the size of a butterfly powered by solar energy, literally a fly on the wall, to mammoth pilotless vehicles like the "Heron" with almost limitless range that can stay in the air for sixty hours and carry satellite navigation systems, a 250-kilogram payload, and sensitive systems, like synthetic-aperture radar, that see through all weather and read and instantaneously analyze electromagnetic-impulse communications. The weapons' systems range from the microtactical to the strategic, from the alleyways of Gaza to outer space. For the infantry who have to fight in close urban environments, like Gaza, with suicide bombers and booby traps in wait, engineers developed the "Mosquito," which looks like a Frisbee, weighs about a pound, has a highly sensitive camera inside, and is used like a boomerang to send back in real time what lies in wait behind corners. Then there are ballistic missiles, developed, designed, and produced in Israel, and the satellites that go with them: unlike other satellites, these are static, all eyes on Hezbollah, Syria, and a few others, but mainly Iran, providing a young major in an intelligence base near Tel Aviv with more information about what is going on in the country at any given time than is known to the Iranian president himself.

Israel's cutting edge is the key to its survival. It has to be one step ahead. In late 2010 the United States was supplying Saudi Arabia with $60 billion in weapons. The United States also makes sure the Egyptian army stays well equipped, and there are advanced American technologies in Pakistan. Many of these weapons are the same as those in Israel's arsenal, like F-15 and F-16 fighters, as well as an array of air-, sea-, and ground-based missile systems. Advanced aircraft are worlds unto themselves, tiny packages of highly condensed technologies all bundled into one. If the Iranians learn the secrets of an F-15's avionics package, or its radars and communications systems, this puts at risk Israel's F-15s, and thus the country's need to make sure the systems in its own aircraft are different and unique. The dual challenges of facing the Iranians and having to improve the world's most sophisticated weapons technologies are what keeps Israel on its toes, constantly having to feed the beast to maintain the leading edge. But there are massive economic payoffs down the line in the educational system that supports it and the economic fruits later reaped. Iran may be a substantial challenge, but of all the others Israel faces, this one seems to be under control and, in a twist, actually benefits Israel.

When the scientists and engineers are released from the military, they become the next generation of Israel's high-tech industrialists, having had the benefit of a challenge, an education, and generous research resources at their disposal for a decade or more. At home there is much criticism of Israel's educational system, but the defense community can always find the several hundred exceptional minds they need each year. If the country was not forced to find and nurture them, the chances are that many would be lost, or neglected.

For Iran to attack Israel is not a simple thing. First there is deterrence: Israel is known to possess an arsenal of several hundred nuclear weapons of various kinds, deliverable in a variety of ways, from submarines to drones, and one assumes that the Iranians have to consider that the punishment Israel alone can mete out, though not as severe or as existential as the blow Israel would sustain, would be "devastating," to quote someone who knows these things intimately. To make it personal, the Iranian leadership knows that no matter how deep the bunker they hide in, they and their families will be eliminated. The Iranians also have to figure that if they attack Israel, the response will not be Israel's alone. The United States is dedicated to Israel's defense, as are key states in Europe. In weighing the cost of attacking Israel, Iran has to take into account the total response.

If deterrence does not work, Iran must factor in that Israel has a proven antimissile system, the Arrow, which allows the country two shots at an incoming missile far enough away from Israel to ensure that any nuclear fallout lands somewhere else. Of course the more missiles Iran can fire, the more problematic interception becomes, and since any one strike against Israel could be fateful, success for Iran is in the numbers. Given the current production rates of fissile materials, Iran will take generations to produce enough nuclear weapons to circumvent the Arrow's defenses, and by then who knows who the leadership of the country will be? So, given the Arrow, even if Iran has a bomb, or even three, it has to take into account that whatever they launch may never reach its target. Yet Israel is not going to wait for nuclear missiles to fall before it reacts. Iran's missiles won't strike home.

Israel is a tiny target. Size counts, but sometimes there is an advantage in being small. The avenues of attack are narrow and defined. Unlike the United States, Israel does not have to patrol borders that are thousands of miles long. Its early-warning satellites, radars, and everything else are entirely focused on some rather narrow corridors.

If the Iranians decide to attack Israel, they will probably use missiles. Even in the best of worlds, missiles can err by a few millidegrees here or there. Such a deviation would see an Iranian missile fall on an Arab country (Lebanon, Jordan, Egypt) or in Gaza, with its massively dense population, the West Bank, or even on Al Aksa Mosque in Jerusalem, Islam's third-holiest site. Half a degree of error is all it would take. Even if the missiles hit Israel itself, the area being so compact, they would poison the waters and land of Palestine for generations to come. Israel's nuclear arsenal, the Arrow, and the problems that narrow defined corridors of advance cause Iran alone should be enough to deter the ayatollahs from sanctioning an attack.

For twenty years now Israel has been trying to stop the Iranian program. In the early 1990s, Amnon Lipkin-Shahak, who was then head of military intelligence and went on to be chief of staff, said in private conversation that if the program went unchecked, the Iranians would have a bomb in eight to ten years. It has taken them more than twice that time, fighting international sanctions, sabotage by the Mossad and CIA, pressure on suppliers, a series of crippling computer viruses, and ongoing harassment by the UN and its agencies. The Tinner family from Switzerland, who allegedly worked for the CIA as early as June 2004 and were key to supplying gas centrifuge technologies to the clients of Pakistani nuclear renegade Abdul Quadeer Khan, including Iran, are suspected by some to have helped the agency sell the Iranians DUD centrifuges, which subsequently exploded in 2006, causing extensive damage to the country's enrichment facility. In February 2007, one of Iran's top nuclear physicists, Ardeshir Husseinpour, a world authority on electromagnetics, died of mysterious radiation poisoning, long suspected fed to him by Israeli intelligence agents. Another top nuclear scientist, Masoud ali Mohammadi, was killed in January 2010 in downtown Teheran when a motorbike exploded near him. Again the Mossad was suspected. In November 2010 the head of the Iranian atomic energy agency, Majid Shahriyari, was killed by a magnetic bomb attached to his car, again in downtown Teheran.

Despite these and other mysterious accidents and deaths, in 2010 the formal assessment of Israeli intelligence and its allies was that once it made the decision to do so, Iran could have a nuclear testable device within "a matter of not too many months," according to a top Israeli authority. It had two main parallel programs going at full steam, enrichment and weaponization, and enough fissile material for two and a half bombs. The country has installed new centrifuges, including two new cascades, clusters

of centrifuges working in unison, at Natanz, the main enrichment facility, many times more effective than the old, and built
new, deeply defended facilities, like the Qom project. The world
will not know for sure whether Iran has a bomb until there is a
test, and as Israel itself showed, there may never be one (though
there were reports of a secret Israel–South Africa test way back
during apartheid).

The suspicion is that Israel would like to attack Iranian facilities
before they become fully operational in bomb production. It would
act alone, as it did when Israeli jets destroyed the Iraqi reactor at
Osirak in 1981, despite the opposition of the world (particularly
the United States, which was supporting Iraq in its war with Iran
at the time), and as Israel did with a nascent Syrian reactor in 2009.
The Iranians know this option is on the table. The Americans
have also repeatedly said that all options on Iran's nuclear program
remain open. The probability of a preemptive strike, however, is
remote. The operational problems involved fill volumes (including
those written by my colleagues at the Institute for National Security
Studies). These include the distance to the targets, the way the re-
actors have been built and fortified underground, air defenses, the
multiple targets that would have to be attacked, the need to spend
long periods over Iranian territory to do the job efficiently, and, of
course, Iranian retaliation, which could range from having agents
poison the ventilator systems of subways around the world with
biotoxins, to having a nuclear suitcase bomb delivered in a container to Ashdod port. It would require a spectacular range of deep-
penetrating bombs to get the job done and after all this, many
experts say, at best Iran's program will be regressed, not stopped.
Others claim it is possible to deliver a deathly blow, depending on

the weapons you are prepared to use, an obtuse reference to tactical nuclear weapons, a possibility no one dares whisper aloud.

Israel cannot attack Iran without some form of coordination with the United States. The distances involved and technological advances made since 1981 in detection equipment will make it almost impossible for Israel to launch an attack without the United States knowing about it. Israel would also have to take into account international outrage, particularly by countries like Russia and China that have worked with the West, albeit reluctantly, to curb the Iranian program and are partners to sanctions on Iran, and by those who may pay the price through terror attacks by Iranian supporters and surrogates for Israel's actions. So there are huge obstacles, military, political, and moral, that make either an Iranian attack on Israel or an Israeli attack on Iran a last-resort scenario. The cost to both countries of such an attack would be vast and enduring. It is strategically nonsensical.

* * *

I sat with Uzi Eilam on the trimmed lawn of his neat garden in one of the older villas in Savyon, a quiet, protected, and exclusive neighborhood just east of Tel Aviv. He made coffee from an espresso machine in a spotless kitchen and brought it out on a tray with a small plate of biscuits. Though he sat there in his ironed short-sleeve checked shirt, jeans, and sandals, he looked like he was still in uniform, still a soldier despite the passage of years. His eyes were twinkly blue, his hair thinning gray, his fingers around the little cup gnarled. He is one of those people you feel it a privilege to be in quiet conversation with; a font of wisdom enriched by experience and history, and in a sense the man who put the David back into the Goliath of the Israeli armed forces. He stirs his coffee with deliberation, his hand steady on the saucer, his modesty belying his past: paratroop officer in the 101 reconnaissance unit commanded by Ariel Sharon, head of the Israeli Atomic Energy Commission, the chief scientist of the defense ministry, head of research in the military, recipient of the highest national awards for his contribution to the country's defense, in charge of Israel's defense relations with Europe, including Russia, and, probably most important, developer of the Talpiot program, which for decades has provided the defense establishment with the brilliant minds it needs. Despite the rank and honors, at heart he remains a simple paratrooper, recounting with great animation and detail the cross-border raids carried out by Unit 101 in the early '50s to try to stop Palestinian Fedayeen terror from coming over the Jordanian border, through to the "good old days" of chasing terrorists in the Jordan Valley in the early 1970s. He was part of a small group of officers that established Israel's first reconnaissance unit to work exclusively for the chief of staff; he was a field intelligence officer, fought in the Sinai campaign, was wounded, and to this day carries the scars on his arm. In 1957, after the Sinai war, he went off to the Technion in Haifa to study electrical engineering and then pursued a second degree in business management at the Hebrew University, with postgraduate studies at Stanford University in California. After a period as a battalion commander in the reserves and a job at an engine production firm in Beit Shemesh, between Jerusalem and Tel Aviv, he went back into the army, this time in weapons development, bringing together his knowledge as a field commander and academic training in engineering and business, and with a deep understanding that to survive, Israel had to be smarter than its enemy. "The math was simple," he said. "Unless we could make one and one make three, we could not win given the disparities between the sides in every dimension: size, population, resources, density, and attitude toward casualties."

In his time the army created a research and development branch of its own, and very smartly sent its scientists to be attached to fighting units to understand the problems firsthand. Eilam's march from Unit 101 to being responsible for Israel's nuclear program by the age of forty is a unique story. But there are many like him, people you meet in the labs and production lines, working on computer screens. In the army one is struck at how young the people are. And in the defense industries there are people like Eilam who possess something unquantifiable, a combination of life experience and science, persecution and perseverance that makes Israel the country it is. Tough, resilient, and resourceful.

"Will that be enough to ensure Israel can survive?" I asked Uzi.

"Oh," he responded, quicker than lightning, "Israel will survive its enemies. I'm optimistic because I know. How it will survive, under what conditions, however, is a whole different story."

And indeed it is.

❦ TWO ❧

New Jew, Old Problem

For over six decades the Israel-Arab conflict has continued in one way or another. The cycle fluctuates from hope to despair and back again. There have been eight full-scale wars between Israel and its neighbors, more than one every decade. These have been punctuated with two increasingly violent intifadas with the Palestinians, the second in which Palestinian suicide bombers claimed almost as many Israeli casualties, killed and wounded, as the 1973 Yom Kippur War, when Israel was taken by surprise on two fronts by two organized, well-trained, Soviet-supplied armies. In 1973 it was Israeli soldiers who paid the price. In the Second Intifada it was civilians, torn to shreds in buses, cinemas, and pedestrian malls.

There have been three peace treaties with the Arabs and Palestinians, countless agreements, and hundreds of meetings, direct and indirect. Peace with Egypt, even before the 2011 uprisings and ouster of President Hosni Mubarak, is cold—there is no shared trade, commerce, or cultural ties—and with Jordan it is dodgy, dependent on the moment. The Oslo agreements with the Palestinians have broken down, and the Palestinians on the West Bank are almost totally cut off from those in Gaza. The West Bank, Israel's card in any negotiations with the Palestinians, has been thoroughly settled with Jews, and there are now so many settlements in what is supposed to be Palestine, one suspects that even Solomon could not find an equitable solution to the conundrum.

How we, the Israelis and Palestinians, got to this point fills library shelves. There is enough justice on both sides to sink the scales of Themis. The Jews, ravaged by history and the Holocaust, saw themselves returning to a land promised to them by the Bible, history, and the United Nations. This, of course, came at the expense of the Palestinians, who, while not a formal nation, were the majority population in the area known as Palestine, at that time under a British mandate.

For the Jews, nationhood was the culmination of a deep desire, held during a history that was peppered with persecution, religion, yearning, schooling, and later political activism. The return to Zion is embedded in the thrice-daily prayers recited by believers, up there with health, prosperity, and obedience before God. However, it took a series of dispersions and pogroms, the publication of the *Protocols of the Elders of Zion*, heinous anti-Semitism, and later the Holocaust to transform the Jews from a liturgical people into a Zionist movement. A new Jew was created, the pioneer, who traded the black garb of the ghetto for khaki shorts and a shirt with as many buttons open as possible, farming first land bought from absentee Turkish effendis who became rich for life selling Galilee swamps to the Jews, and later fertile fields purchased by philanthropists who were also harnessed to a political process that saw first the 1917 Balfour Declaration, then the 1947 UN Partition Plan that gave birth to the Jewish state.

The Arabs declared war the day after Israel declared independence on May 15, 1948. The Arab states, adamantly opposed to the creation of a Western foothold in Arabia, made the Palestinians a cause before the Palestinians even knew they had a cause. Egypt, Iraq, Jordan, Lebanon, and Syria attacked Israel on four fronts with vastly superior armies, yet managed to lose the war. At least that is the narrative one is taught in Jewish schools: that the Arabs vastly outnumbered the Jews; the Jews had no formal military experience and were armed with only a few old rifles from Czechoslovakia, but courage and resourcefulness saved the day.

The truth is somewhat different. The Jews were quite well equipped to meet the war. From their very first tentative steps in the region the Arabs, and later the British, had been at their throats. In 1909 they established the Hashomer—Watchman—unit; its members dressed like Arabs but looked and behaved like Cossacks. Their primary purpose was to protect Jewish settlements from Arab thieves, much more of a problem at the time than Palestinian nationalism. In 1920, after a series of Arab riots, the loosely organized Hashomer was brought under one command, the Haganah—Defense—which continued to operate on a regional rather than a national basis. But continued riots, increasingly widespread and violent in nature like those in Jaffa in 1921, and the August 1929 massacres in Safed and Hebron, led to a consolidation of the Haganah and its restructuring so that by 1936 it could field 10,000 men and had an additional 40,000 in reserves.

In 1941, the British initially encouraged and trained an elite force of 2,000 commandoes, the Palmach, that they hoped would be able to help stop any move by the Axis countries to cross Palestine, but abruptly stopped doing so when they realized that they were actually training the core of the Israeli army-to-be. The Palmach's five battalions were schooled in the military skills that had brought the British across the jungles of Burma and the deserts of North Africa. Each man was carefully selected for physical and mental prowess. They were given leadership tasks and infused with the mores that made the British army a great fighting force. They were taught ingenuity, survival techniques, navigation, stealth, and a code of honor that left no man, wounded or dead, in enemy territory. The Palmach provided the Haganah with the leadership and battle skills it needed, and by the time the Arabs arrived in 1948, they found not a bunch of shivering Jews waiting for the slaughter but a well-trained, well-armed, and well-commanded army. In addition to its intake of 2,000 command-quality fighters from the Palmach, the army would benefit from the 30,000 Jews who served with Allied forces during the Second World War, 5,000 in the Jewish Brigade alone, who came into the ranks of the Haganah: British-trained pilots and naval officers, Russian artillery and armor experts, and saboteurs trained in the Irgun and Lehi undergrounds. There were fighters who had been honed in resistance movements fighting the Nazis and their allies all over Europe, people who had seen the worst and knew how to survive. Even the new recruits the Arabs would face, new immigrants of serving age, taken straight from the ships, given a rifle, and put in the battlefield, were battle-hardened like few others. They had survived the Holocaust.

The Arabs initially invaded with a combined force of 23,000, commanded by four different general staffs, without a unified plan other than to cross the border, find Jews wherever they could, and push them back into the sea. They had not prepared for this war, totally underestimated the Jews, and were confident that the hundreds of thousands of Palestinians inside what the Jews called Israel would rise up with them, like an unstoppable fifth column, or fifth force. They were wrong on all counts.

As early as 1946 Israel's first prime minister, David Ben Gurion, had begun building the armed forces he knew Israel would need to survive the Arab onslaught that would surely come. Resources were invested in expanding underground arms-producing industries to making millions of bullets and hundreds of thousands of grenades and mortar shells a year. A mass buying spree, focused on the mounds of postwar weapons available on the black market, brought in enough rifles, machine guns, and other weapons to arm almost every recruit and to allow Tzahal, the Israel Defense Forces (IDF), as the Haganah was now called, to establish classic battle formations with the appropriate weaponry. In December 1947 compulsory service was instituted, later extended to all men under forty, most of whom managed to receive formal training and were placed according to skills in a military architecture that included all the basic elements of a modern fighting machine, including communications, extensive infrastructure left over by the British air, armor, and artillery units, some mechanized infantry, and a fighting spirit that surprised even the Jews.

The key, however, was the extensive battle experience the commanders of the young Israeli forces had accrued prior to the establishment of the state. The commander of the critical central front, Moshe Dayan, lost his eye fighting the Vichy French in Lebanon together with the 7th Australian Brigade in 1941. Yigael Yadin, the head of operations, had been in the Haganah since 1932, and directed many of its most successful operations. Responsible for training the IDF's officers' corps and the army's logistics was Haim Laskov, who had served with Orde Wingate's Night Squads, fought the Nazis in Germany, graduated from the British army with the rank of major, and worked for Aliya Bet saving Jewish refugees from Europe. The chief of staff, wise and seasoned Yaakov Dori, left Ukraine after the 1905 pogrom, completed high school at the Reali in Haifa, joined the Jewish Legion of the British army in World War I, headed the Haganah in problematic Haifa with its sizable Arab population, and since 1939, under the close watch of Ben Gurion, had been building the Israel Defense Forces, bringing together the Haganah, Palmach, and Jewish undergrounds into one cohesive, disciplined army serving the new sovereign government of the Jewish state. Together they were formidable.

In May 1948, ten days after the Arabs opened fire, Israel had twelve organized infantry and armored divisions. In addition, thousands of volunteers, Jewish and non-Jewish, flooded into Israel, many graduates of action in World War II. Of the Israel air force's 205 pilots, 180 were volunteers from 15 countries, some of whom could not speak the same language, not an uncommon problem at the time.

The War of Independence, as Israel calls it, or the Nakba, "catastrophe," in Palestinian terminology, left 6,372 Israelis dead, almost 1 percent of the Jewish population of pre-state Palestine, more deaths than in all of Israel's other wars combined.

The Arabs were defeated, but it was the Palestinians who paid a huge price for the war. Over 700,000 of the 950,000 Palestinians in Jewish-held Palestine fled the country or were expelled. An additional 160,000 left homes for what they thought would be temporary safe havens in the Arab-populated Galilee. Their exile became permanent, however, when the areas to which they fled fell back into Israel territory under the 1949 armistice agreement that ended the war. To this day they have not been allowed back to their original homes and are classified as "present absentees," in a miraculous feat of bureaucratic dexterity, which makes them refugees and Israeli Arab citizens at the same time.

Those Palestinians left in Israel were tolerated and given os-tensibly the same political freedoms as the Jews, and were the beneficiaries of the only democracy in the Middle East. They were kept under military rule in many parts of the country, how-ever, and government allocations were discriminatory and be-grudging. The secret service kept an open eye on their actions. Israeli Arabs were denied government jobs and not allowed to do military service, a key to employment opportunities and sub-sidies in Israel at the time. Law and order in the Arab villages that remained was kept via a system of patronage, where village elders were given government cash to hand out in return for clan quiescence and guarantees of bloc voting for the Mapai ruling party in the next election. Where carrots didn't work, sticks were used, including house demolitions, martial law, and arrest under the draconian emergency laws the British had left behind, which the Israelis were quick to adopt. This, coupled with the general state of shell shock the Palestinians left in Israel were in, kept things generally quiet.

But it was different in the Arab countries. They had an interest in keeping the Palestinian refugee issue alive, on the surface to ensure the Palestinians got their homeland back, but in fact to keep them out of their own delicate sociopolitical realities at this time. Neither Jordan nor Egypt wanted a sudden influx of Palestinians to add to their own problems. Egypt was way overpopulated and Jordan, in the tenuous hands of the Hashemite Kingdom, did not want more non-Hashemite Palestinians to threaten the throne or move Jordan in directions the kingdom preferred to avoid. The Egyptians kept the Palestinians in refugee camps in Gaza, placing them under curfew and under the careful eye of the Mukhabarat, Egypt's efficient intelligence agency. They were denied freedom of movement and citizenship. The Egyptians built no schools or infrastructure. It was all left up to the UN in the form of UNRWA, the United Nations Relief and Works Agency for Palestinian Refugees in the Near East, which continues to assist the Palestinian refugees more than sixty years later.

The Palestinians who fled to Jordan had it somewhat better, at least until 1967, when 160,000 of them were made refugees again when Israel conquered the West Bank. In September 1970, when the Palestinians tried to set up an independent army in Jordan, the king's campaign of retribution was merciless. Tens of thousands were expelled once again, this time to Lebanon, Iraq, and beyond, to be denied citizenship, land ownership, and free professional choice, and becoming victims in a whole series of conflicts, some not of their own making, but in which they always paid the price.

The Israel that the Arabs had attacked was not what it seemed on paper. It was a nation of one-third Holocaust survivors, people who had been to hell's door and back and lived by the motto "never again." After surviving the Nazis and their willing anti-Semitic cronies, the Arabs did not seem like an insurmountable challenge. Hardly a family in Israel at the time had not been touched by the Holocaust. The main body of Jews from Arab lands was still to come, and the population was almost entirely of European origin, from the shtetls and ghettos wiped from the face of the earth by the Nazis who made them dig their own graves there before mowing them down, naked, in after-breakfast sport. The stories once heard in whispers were arriving loud and clear as people with firsthand testimony made it through the British blockades to Israel's shores. "Never again" became the national mantra. Had the Arabs just accepted the Jewish state as delineated by the 1947 UN Partition Plan, the trauma of the Holocaust may have dissipated with time. The combined Arab attack accomplished the opposite. It only strengthened it. The survival syndrome permeated every level of society, paranoia was seen as a national value, great freedoms were afforded the security organizations, generals were Israel's soccer stars, and the secret service, the silent heroes of the day. If postwar Jewish survival was forged in the ovens of Hitler, it was galvanized by the 1948 war.

The 1949 armistice agreement left Israel with temporary borders looking like an inflated kidney, only nine miles wide in the middle, and with Jerusalem divided. Much of the land, the Negev, was barren. Two key Jewish symbols, Hebron and the Old City of Jerusalem, fell into Jordanian hands. The king's troops had been trained and commanded by the British. The Galilee to the north was heavily populated by Arabs, the border with Lebanon long and undulating through heavy bush and dense forests. The Syrians were encamped on the Golan Heights, leaving Israeli settlements in the northern Galilee in their palm, able to be shelled at random from the steep ridges above.

Israel's main water sources, the snows of the Hermon on the Golan, and the Hazbani and Litani Rivers that flowed into the Jordan from Lebanon and from there into Lake Kinneret, were in enemy territory. The Syrians had their hands on Israel's main tap and could close it at will. Water was also an issue between Israel and Jordan, with the two sharing water sources that met at the confluence of the Israeli, Jordanian, and Syrian borders at Mevo Hama. Moving a rock this way or that could change the flow dramatically either in Israel's direction or toward the Jordan River and Jordan's breadbasket in the Jordan Valley. The new status quo could not be expected to last for long.

 THREE

The Melting Pot

While the Palestinians became eternal refugees, by 1949 Israel's population grew from 650,000 to one million. Ten years later, in 1958, it doubled to two million, immigrants arriving from over a hundred countries. In 1950 the Law of Return was legislated, affording automatic Israeli citizenship to anyone who was one-eighth Jewish, the same criterion the Nazis used to feed the gas ovens. That year, in a remarkable operation commonly known as "Magic Carpet" but code-named "On Eagles' Wings" from a verse from the prophet Isaiah, almost the entire Yemenite Jewish community was transported to Israel in 380 secret flights from Aden, made public only months after the operation ended. A year later, in 1951, 120,000 Jews were airlifted to Israel from Iraq in operations Ezra and Nehemiah, again code-named after the prophets, as if what was happening was nothing short of their biblical prophecies coming to fruition. An additional 100,000 were brought from Poland and Rumania. Since the Jewish agency was paying thousands of dollars for each Jew released, superficially these countries were asking Israel to pay them back for the education those emigrating had received. In fact, it was nothing other than a head tax, practically a ransom. In addition, all property was left behind by those emigrating and subsequently was confiscated by the state.

The trauma of the people reaching Israel immediately after 1948 was universal in terms of suffering. Almost to a person they came penniless and humiliated. Egypt and Libya expelled their Jews, while the twenty other Arab-speaking countries, other than Lebanon, did everything they could to ensure the Jews would leave as quickly as possible: there were hangings for alleged spying for Israel, property confiscations, curfews, and the closing down of schools and synagogues.

As many Jews, between 800,000 and a million, fled Arab countries as Palestinians fled Israel in 1948, abandoning property valued in today's terms at $300 billion. Of those, 680,000 came to Israel; the rest, particularly the wealthy, opted for France, Italy, and other more peaceful parts of the world.

Even in Israel there is little real understanding of the trauma faced by the Jews forced to leave Arab lands, of once-aristocratic families, Jews living like pashas and effendis, deprived of all their possessions, banished and absorbed by an impoverished nation fighting for its life with very little to give other than the rudimentary supplies for getting by.

A close friend, Eli, once told me of his family in Egypt, where his father owned two pharmacies, of their home in Zamalek, Cairo's posh quarter, and their summer home in "Alex." The family enjoyed a driver, a gardener, maids, and private lessons. There had been ups and downs with the Egyptians, especially during the war years when the Egyptians, in order to rid themselves of the British, joined forces with the Germans, but all in all his life was one of prosperity, religious freedom, and culture.

Things changed radically with the birth of Israel and the ascent of Gamal Abdel Nasser, who was determined to be the leader of a pan-Arab world animated by the extinction of Israel and expulsion of the West as its cause.

In 1956 Egypt forcibly expelled its Jews. Within a decade a thirty-two-century presence of the Jewish community in Egypt was whittled down to fewer than a thousand people. In all, more than 65,000 people were forced in one way or another to leave their homes.

In Eli's memory they had but minutes to leave, taking with them only what they could carry. At Port Said, the western end of the Suez Canal, they were herded onto a ship like cattle. Egyptian soldiers who boarded the boat made Eli's mother take the rings off her fingers and from her throat a necklace, a wedding present from her husband's grandmother that had been in the family for generations. He remembered their chaotic arrival in Israel, the temporary camp near Lod, where the family was taken, assigned a tent, given a shower, heavily dosed with white DDT bug-killing powder, and given rough khaki clothes. He remembers more than anything the humiliation of his father, that authoritative patriarch of the family, reduced to nothing in front of his eyes. The Jews of Europe came decimated; the Jews from Arab lands, impoverished, confused, and bitter.

There is no underestimating the social and psychological degradation suffered by the Sephardim when they first arrived in the country. The first generation was lost. Patriarchal systems broke down as children worked to support parents who could not speak the language or find jobs in their trades and professions. And often in families of six children or more, the second generation was lost as well, destined to menial jobs in factories, built almost as charity in the new development towns being hastily constructed to solidify Israel's hold on the land along the borders and at strategic junctions internally, or to a life of crime, drug abuse, and alcoholism.

To deal with the influx, the State of Israel's early leaders engineered a Zionist socialist economy that provided as much as it could for the Jews like Eli's family and as little as was respectable for the Israeli Arabs. The camps Eli remembers, the Ma'abarot, were a blight on those who built them and a social curse for the tens of thousands who went through them. It was an indelible experience on their transition from the Diaspora to Israel and a scar of resentment the Sephardim bore toward the Labor governments in Israel from that time on.

Their arrival, on the other hand, ended the hegemony of the kibbutz movement and the socialist Labor Party in the land. It would take twenty years and two wars before their vote would determine the future course of Israel, and only then by the election of a most improbable candidate, Menachem Begin, a Polish gentleman, to lead them.

Begin, a unique personality—brilliant orator, fierce revisionist, always polite, yet a former terrorist commander—understood that he could not sell the Sephardim the philosophies of his hero and mentor, Ze'ev Jabotinsky, the founder of Zionist Revisionism. But he could capitalize on their hatred and mistrust of the Arabs who expelled them, and the "Mapainikim," as the Labor-led socialist government was called, who kept the Sephardim simmering in tents while they allegedly feathered their own nests.

In what they had considered a magnanimous gesture, the Mapainikim, when putting their cabinets together in smoke-filled rooms, reserved just two ministerial posts for the Sephardim: those of posts and police. Anything to do with defense, finance, development, or school syllabus was left to the "real" leaders, the *vatikim*, old-timers who had built the country.

But too much criticism of those who absorbed the masses is ill-placed. With no detailed research, it would seem nothing short of a miracle that a country fresh out of a war absorbed twice its population when most of the new arrivals came with nothing but a suitcase and heavy psychological baggage. The country fed, educated, and housed them. There was no hunger in the land. There was a good health system and centralized distribution of fresh produce to every corner. A cooperative bus company, Egged, provided regular service to communities in the middle of nowhere. Development towns were built from the ground up, with kindergartens, schools, community centers, and parks.

It was not a paradise and in the haste, massive mistakes were made, such as congregating poverty in certain areas and placing Jews from countries like Yemen, where their main trade was as silversmiths, on cooperative farms in the Jerusalem hills with a few chickens and telling them to make a living. But with time, the chickens came with expert advice and heavy subsidies to build modern runs for egg and poultry production. A centralized distribution arm, Tnuva, made sure the produce conformed to health standards and that it was sold and distributed efficiently.

Those with cows went through the same process. The established kibbutzim sometimes helped their new neighbors, though the extent of this remains contested to this day. But often the cultural gap was too wide to breach. Once, when I was eighteen, I drove a kibbutz veterinarian to see a sick cow on a nearby moshav, a collective agricultural settlement, in the Eila Valley, near where David killed Goliath. The sick cow, their only cow, had been moved into the children's bedroom and the nine children to the small lounge that also served as a dining room. The vet later explained that one could always have more children, whereas the cow both provided sustenance and cost money to replace. There was no question that it deserved the bedroom.

It is also nothing short of remarkable how the Hebrew language was developed and taught, and the youth, for the most part, molded into a new society. A unique Hebrew-teaching system, the *ulpan*, was set up across the country to replace whatever language the new immigrants had brought with them. In some cases little tolerance was shown to those who did not toe the line. In the 1950s, when the famous Yiddish actors the Burnsteins tried to stage a Shalom Aleichem play in Yiddish in Jerusalem, the police closed the show down, arrested the actors, and fined the producer.

Ben Gurion envisioned the army as the country's "melting pot," the national kitchen where the multiple ingredients flowing into the country could be mixed with the language, values, comradeship, and Zionist commitment to make them into "New Jews," Yitzhak Rabin and Yigal Allon types: smart, good-looking, confident, able to defend themselves, and with just the right intonation to their spoken Hebrew to make it sound like their native language. And so it was. The army became the great national socializer, taking in young men and women from varied backgrounds and turning them into one unified corps, dedicated to democracy and their Jewish heritage, though not necessarily to the Jewish religion.

With all its shortcomings, failures, and arrogance, the absorption of Israel's Jews was contrapuntal to the Palestinian experience. For the Jews it was a homecoming, for the Palestinians expulsion; for the Jews it brought citizenship and acceptance, for the Palestinians rejection and discrimination; for the Jews victory, for the Palestinians defeat; for the Jews a future of hope in a new land, for the Palestinians entry into a long tunnel with no light visible at the end. The 1948 war set the stage, leaving the Palestinians dissipated and weak, with those under Israeli rule compliant, resentful, suspicious, and mainly confused. They were regarded with some degree of contempt by the Arabs and Palestinians who fled, almost as quislings, especially those who cooperated with the Israeli government. There was an interesting debate in the country at the time, according to one of my colleagues at the Institute for National Security Studies, Nachman Tal, a former acting head of the secret service. He recalls that the security community strongly recommended that Israeli Arabs quickly be brought into the civil service and even the foreign ministry. The secret service argued that the best way to deal with the issue was to integrate the Arabs into both the political system and the government bureaucracy, just as the Ottomans and British had done before them. The advice was ignored. Still, the Israeli Arabs have not come out too badly. In every poll conducted, when asked whether, as Israeli Arabs, they would rather live in Palestine than Israel, over 85 percent opt for the Jewish state.

Of course, like so much else about this story, the result is somewhat disingenuous. Ask Israeli Arabs whether they would like to see a Palestinian state occupy the territory between the Mediterranean and the Jordan River, and the answer would surely hover around the 100 percent mark.

No matter what the polls say, Israeli Arabs are Palestinians who happen to live in Israel. Israel is not a country whose borders they forged, nor did they have anything to do with establishing its national institutions or founding ethos. They were not consulted in its development and though free to vote and be active members in Israel's Knesset, or parliament, the closest they could come in terms of expressing themselves politically in the first decades of the state was through a mainly Jewish-led Communist Party. Their new flag was the blue Jewish Star of David on a white background, with two blue stripes running parallel to the flag's top and bottom borders, to represent the tallith, the shawl a Jew wears when praying. The national anthem, they were told, was "Hatikvah," or "hope," written by Naphtali Herz Imber, a Galician Jew from Zolochiv, in the 1880s, who did not quite have the Palestinians in mind when he wrote:

As long as in the heart, within,
A Jewish soul still yearns,
And onward, towards the end of the east,
An eye still gazes toward Zion.
Our hope is not yet lost,
The hope of 2,000 years,
To be a free people in our land,
The land of Zion and Jerusalem.
(Twice repeated)

If the War of Independence, the Nakba, was traumatic for the Palestinians and Arabs, the 1967 Six-Day War was a thunderbolt that once again showed how distant Israel was from an existential threat. Its survival was never seriously at risk. The war was sparked by Nasser's decision to expel UN peacekeepers from positions along the Israeli-Gaza border, and threats to close the Tiran Straits in southern Sinai to Israeli shipping. Passage through the straits was vital for Israel's oil supplies from then-friendly Iran to the port in Eilat, and for its commerce with Africa and the Far East.

Israel's victory was stunning. Despite much dithering, Israeli premier Levi Eshkol, an uncharismatic technocrat who succeeded Ben Gurion in 1963, with no pretentions of filling the great man's shoes, gave in to his generals: the charismatic Moshe Dayan, hero of the 1956 Sinai campaign, now minister of defense; Ezer Weizman, the fast-talking, fast-shooting, indefatigable former air force head and now head of military planning and operations; and a quiet, taciturn, socially uneasy, chain-smoking Yitzhak Rabin, who was chief of staff. All sabras, born in Israel, they were absolutely sure about what Israel had to do to survive: attack, take the initiative, counter numbers with ingenuity, take the enemy by surprise, and wreak enough destruction on the Arab armed forces to ensure this was the last war for a long time to come.

In two days Jordan, Iraq, Egypt, and Syria saw their air forces destroyed; a few days later Israeli forces, including me, got to the Suez Canal, as well as Jerusalem, the Jordan River, and the unassailable Golan Heights and Hermon Mountain. Israel's victory was total. Smoldering wrecks, acrid smoke, dazed prisoners of war, horribly burned corpses, and landscapes that now resembled the moon were what remained of the battle zones. The Arab armies were humiliated. On the Golan Heights Israeli soldiers found Syrian infantrymen chained to their posts while their officers had fled.

Again, military casualties aside, the main victims were the Palestinians. Over 300,000 people fled their homes in Gaza and on the West Bank to become refugees in Jordan, Lebanon, Syria, Iraq, and anywhere that would take them. For almost half, 145,000, this was their second exile. Again, twenty years after 1948, they found themselves in a war in which they had no part, had not asked for, and had nothing to do with Palestinian interests. The rest ended up under Israeli occupation. The 1967 war was not about liberating Palestine, but about Nasser and pan-Arabism. The Palestinians were not party to the decision to go to war. The Straits of Tiran were hundreds of miles from Palestine, so they had no interests there. The Palestinians had no air force and no army, and posed no threat to anyone. How ironic then that the Palestinians would become Israel's greatest nemesis, and Israel's occupation of the territories the stepping stone of the Palestinian people toward their own independence.

 FOUR

Entanglement

Victory in the Six-Day War was the first hitch in the Gordian knot that now ties Israel and the Palestinians. It doomed the sides to a clash of nationalisms that has become more vociferous and intractable with time. Israel's problem after 1967 was that it wanted the territory, but not the almost one million Arabs who came with it. Some wanted to keep it for biblical, historical reasons, others for strategic reasons. There was a consensus that Jerusalem would never be divided again, nor would Israel relinquish what it considered its sovereign rights to the holy sites in the Old City. For many this was a giddy time, a time when the yoke of the ghetto, the shame of the Holocaust, was shed and a sense of invincibility set in, even Messianic redemption as Jews flooded to the Western Wall and the Machpelah in Hebron where Abraham and the other patriarchs and matriarchs are buried, the cornerstones of the Jewish belief whose names are central to almost every prayer.

The Palestinians were immediately placed under military law with a military administration governed by the same emergency regulations used by the British, but without the death sentence. Beyond that, no one in Israel had any clear idea of what to do. The demographic threat, as it has now become recognized, was lost in the euphoria of the moment. Ben Gurion, however, saw the writing on the wall: immediately after the war, he told Israel to shed the territories as quickly as possible before the Jews became a minority in their own land.

Moshe Dayan considered himself Ben Gurion's protégé. He should have listened to the "Old Man." Instead, he was dazzled by victory. As defense minister, he was responsible for the territories. As a war hero, his advice was considered sacrosanct. He spoke fluent Arabic and was supposed to have a deep understanding of Arabic culture. Since he was the strategist who had brought the greatest military success to the people of Israel since David killed Goliath, the country looked to him for a solution.

Dayan, and the other young leaders in the cabinet like Yigal Allon, the former commander of the Palmach and now deputy prime minister, pushed for a policy that would keep those areas of strategic importance in Israel's hands and would limit Jewish settlement of the territories to what was necessary for military needs alone, far from any Palestinian population concentrations. They believed that economic integration was the key, backed by a strong military administration and draconian restrictions to ensure compliance. The Palestinians were not seen as a nation. Their fate was to be decided in talks with the Jordanians and the Egyptians, if ever. Ironically, when peace was eventually made with both Jordan and Egypt, they did so on the condition that

Israel kept the occupied territories and the Palestinians with them, apparently for good reason.

The Israeli government sought to impose basically the same structure that had "worked" with the Israeli Arabs, fragmenting leadership on a village-by-village, town-by-town basis with a system of patronage that encouraged clans to blunt any Palestinian nationalism that emerged.

Initially it seemed to work. After Eshkol's death in 1969, Golda Meir became the country's fourth prime minister, only the third woman in the world to attain such a high position. In interviews with the *Sunday Times* of London and the *Washington Post* on the second anniversary of the Six-Day War, she bluntly said that there was no such thing as a Palestinian, that there were no Palestinian people, and that Israel had taken no territory away from the Palestinians, because they never had any territory to begin with. She, too, was blinded by Israel's power, to the extent that she became one of Israel's most myopic leaders ever. She never saw the possibility for peace when President Anwar Sadat extended his hand through Nahum Goldman, the head of the World Zionist Congress in the early 1970s, and she never saw the oncoming war in 1973, even though the writing on the wall could not have been clearer. Though she claimed to represent a left-wing party, in truth it was anything but. Maybe in terms of some last rudiments of socialism that survived, she and her government could be called leftist. When it came to territory, however, Meir's government had all the arrogance of the old colonials. The Green Line, the 1949 armistice demarcation, was defiantly erased. Dayan spoke about the need to keep Sinai, from El Arish on the Mediterranean to Sharm el-Sheikh at the entrance to the Red Sea, while Yigal Allon offered the Allon Plan, which incorporated into Israel all of the Judean desert, the hills to the east of Jerusalem, and chunks of the West Bank.

To stake Israel's claim to historic Hebron, Allon in 1970 built Kiryat Arba on the outskirts, setting a new model for Israeli settlement and the continued occupation and domination of more than 150,000 Palestinians who lived in the city. The name Kiryat Arba was not coincidental. If anything, it was indicative of Allon's real motives: reclamation of the holy land. According to the Book of Joshua, Kiryat Arba, the burial place of the patriarchs and matriarchs, was the original name of Hebron. Today Kiryat Arba is home to memorial parks for Rabbi Meir Kahane and Baruch Goldstein, the rabbi's disciple who gunned down 29 Muslims and injured 150 more in the 1994 Hebron mosque massacre. Not exactly what the "left wing" had planned for the town, one can suppose.

Menachem Begin, Golda Meir's right-wing successor, made no pretentions about what he wanted: the immediate and total annexation of all territories taken in the Six-Day War. He called it a liberation, not an occupation, seeing it as another step toward the realization of Jabotinsky's dream of a Hebrew state on both sides of the Jordan.

Begin took power following the failures of the Labor government in the 1973 war. People wanted change and Begin certainly offered that. He spoke about the reallocation of resources away from the fat-cat socialists who pretended they had a social conscience. He was for an open market and an end to the iron control the labor unions had on the country. Above all, he was going to reclaim biblical Judea and Samaria, the modern West Bank, for the Jews, leaving Gaza and the Golan as potential bargaining chips for the future. As for the Palestinians, as a true democrat and stickler for legality, Begin suggested extending Israeli citizenship to the inhabitants of liberated Judea, Samaria, and Gaza, as he called the occupied territories, not understanding for a minute the demographic consequences of doing so. At the time, Israel's two million Jews had an annual growth rate of 1.6 percent. The 1.2 million Palestinians in Israel and the occupied territories, the West Bank and Gaza, were growing at more than double that. The Palestinians in Gaza boasted the then highest birthrate in the world outside of Africa, over 4 percent. (Now the Negev Bedouin have surpassed that, with men having as many as three or four "sisters" in addition to their wives—polygamy is officially illegal in Israel—and up to thirty children, all of whom are social security beneficiaries till the age of eighteen; not a bad cottage industry. By 2020, it is estimated, the Bedouin will number 400,000 souls.)

Today there is virtual parity between the 5.7 million Jews and 5.4 million Arabs in Israel and the territories. With the population of Gaza doubling every ten years and the birthrate on the West Bank a full percentile point higher than that of Jewish Israelis, numerical equality between them will soon be reached, after which the Palestinians will surpass the Jews.

It took almost thirty years—between Begin's mulling giving the Palestinians Israeli citizenship and another Likud leader, Ariel Sharon—to realize that demography was Israel's biggest enemy. In August 2005, Sharon unilaterally pulled Israel out of Gaza in a wrenching move that saw the first sparks of a potential civil war in Israel, because he knew he had shed 1.5 million Palestinians from the scales. Sharon uprooted twenty-one settlements in Gaza and incurred the wrath of the Right, who claimed that he was selling out his mentor, Menachem Begin. If he had remained true to Begin, however, and if Begin had had his way in 1977, there technically would be no democratic Jewish state. Instead, in the best case, we would have a binational state, or as the Palestinians and Israeli Arabs call it, a state for all its citizens with an end to Jewish dominance. Some Israelis see this as a model as well, the implications of which are that the Jews would become a minority in their own country.

FIVE

Death to
the Peacemakers

Peacemaking, which should bring security, has proved perilous. Anwar Sadat was assassinated by Islamic fundamentalists on October 6, 1981, while taking the salute at a military parade in honor of Egypt's recapture of the Suez Canal from Israel eight years before. Four years earlier, on November 19, 1977, in an unforgettable gesture that left many in Israel with tears in their eyes, Sadat landed majestically at Ben Gurion airport, proceeded to Jerusalem, and extended his hand in peace to the Jewish people.

Menachem Begin, Israel's right-wing prime minister, the nationalist, made peace with Egypt and was prepared to sacrifice Israeli control over the Sinai because he believed it would allow him to keep the occupied West Bank, which he called Judea and Samaria and which he considered Israel's biblical right, and the Golan Heights, which he considered critical for Israel's security.

And, with Egypt, the most powerful Arab nation, out of the way, Israel could concentrate more forces on imposing the occupation and could transfer money from the defense budget to building the settlements in the territories, which he saw as stakes in Israel's claim to Eretz Yisrael, the Land of Israel.

Begin did not die because of peace, however. It was the first Lebanese war that killed him, a war he never wanted and whose dimensions he did not understand until it was too late. Sharon, his nemesis-protégé, lied to him and manipulated him into Israel's worst military disaster since the Yom Kippur War a decade before. The first Lebanese war, in 1982, started with limited objectives against the Palestine Liberation Organization in south Lebanon, where Israel was being shelled with growing regularity, before growing into a campaign that took Israeli forces to the center of Beirut and beyond, sparked a conflict with the Syrians, and culminated in the Sabra and Shatila massacres by Israeli Phalangist allies in September 1982, leading to Sharon's dismissal as defense minister and Begin's decline into a slow and agonizing death. In the first year of the war, 17,825 Lebanese, who had nothing to do with it, were killed, and an additional 30,000 were wounded. Some 2,000 armed Palestinians were killed, and the rest of the PLO's military core exiled to Tunis with Yasser Arafat, their leader, in August 1982. Israel suffered 368 dead, an unimaginable number to Begin when he had given his initial permission to act against the Palestinians in Lebanon in early June 1982, in response to a Palestinian assassination attempt on Israel's ambassador in London. The people of Israel who thought this was a limited excursion became alarmed by its dimensions and disgusted by Israel's part in the massacres in the Sabra and Shatila refugee camps south of

Beirut, a two-day spree in which at least 800 unarmed civilians were killed. Over 400,000 Israelis, the largest single congregation of people there, crowded into the Tel Aviv Municipal Square to protest, and a vigil was started outside Begin's Jerusalem home with a tally board giving the ever-changing number of Israelis being killed. One of his closest aides, Yehiel Kadishai, admitted once that the war had crippled Begin, but the scoreboard outside his bedroom window had killed him.

Yitzhak Rabin, the chief of general staff who oversaw Israel's victory in the 1967 Six-Day War, was not to die on the battle-field or as a result of pangs of guilt over wasted lives in an ill-conceived war. He was a tragic victim of the peace process and the first to show how the Palestinian issue had the capacity to corrode Israel's moral center. Rabin was a strategic hawk who flew in the direction of peace, looked physically ill when shaking hands with Arafat on the White House lawn in September 1993 upon sealing the Oslo Accords, and seemed to be embracing a friend when he and King Hussein cemented peace between Israel and Jordan in 1994. Rabin was killed by a man now automati-cally referred to as "an Israeli religious fanatic," though Yigal Amir, a law student at Bar Ilan University, was probably less fa-natical than many assume. He was very much part of a culture that taught that territory was holy, that the government of Israel was illegitimate and its leaders, traitors—*mosrim*, a biblical term with deep religious connotations, including a virtual license to kill. Rabin was assassinated on November 4, 1995, after singing the "Song of Peace" with tens of thousands of others celebrating peace in the same municipal square where the Sabra and Shatila protests had taken place fifteen years before. Amir shot Rabin in the back as he was leaving, and the prime minister was declared dead by his aide Eitan Haber a few hours later, in an announcement broadcast to the world while Haber held a blood-soaked page with the words to the "Song of Peace" on it.

Rabin's decision in 1993 to sign the Camp David Accords with Arafat was a decision of last resort. With a stable peace with Egypt and a state of non-belligerency with Jordan (peace was soon to follow) and Syria, Rabin wanted to close the circle by resolving the most intractable issue of all: the future of the occupied territories. As a general, he once told me in an interview, he had always fought for peace; now he felt it was his duty to deliver it. It was in the line of duty that he died for it. In wars he had to overcome the enemy. Here he had to overcome half his own people, opposed to the Oslo Accords and to the handing over of any territories to the eventual independent Palestinian entity, presumed to be a state, specified as the end product of the agreements.

Yigal Amir was no fanatic. Israeli politics was incredibly ugly at the time, constantly at a boiling point, enflamed by the Right and religious nationalists who, each for their own reason, believed Rabin was about to sacrifice Israel on the altar of Palestinian nationalism. The security-minded saw the territory as a strategic asset; others believed it better to keep the Palestinians under one's thumb rather than independent and preparing for the next round of war against the Jewish state. Then there was God. Dozens of rabbis who had spoken to Him recently preached that giving up the land of the fathers was a sin and against His will. The second- and third-generation settlers, the youngsters, knew nothing of the Green Line, could not tell you where the 1967 boundaries were, and had been brought up and educated in a bubble that let little of the outside world creep in, believed that Rabin was giving away their promised birthright, Eretz Yisrael, God's land. When he assassinated Rabin, Amir had enough rabbis backing him to secure a place in heaven had he been killed carrying out his mission. As sure as day follows night, almost instantaneously there would have been a memorial park in his name, with a monument in Kiryat Arba, next to those of Goldstein and Kahane, yet another pilgrimage point.

Rabin's assassination was, however, for almost everybody an act of going too far. The backlash against the settlers from the general Israeli public was enormous, and self-criticism was, in some places, deep and sincere, particularly among the vanishing elderly Revisionists who shared Begin's views on political correctness. But there was also the flip side, those who said that it was God's hand that had struck down Rabin, that it was a warning for anyone who even considered the idea again, that it may have been Amir's finger on the trigger, but the gun was in the hand of Providence.

And so it was. The assassination ended any real chance of peace at that time between the Israelis and Palestinians. Rabin and Arafat did not like each other, but there was a mutual respect that counted for a lot. Arafat knew that Rabin saw through him and he went into the Oslo process knowing that Rabin would not be around forever, Israeli politics being as volatile as they were at the time, and that for ultimate victory in his battle for the liberation of Palestine and the return of the refugees, he needed to proceed one step at a time. Oslo gave Arafat a foothold in Palestine, established him as the undisputed leader of the Palestinian people, and consolidated all Palestinian budgets into his purse, to which he exclusively held the strings. It brought him international legitimacy and restored him in the eyes of the Arabs who had plenty of reasons to despise him. Most important, it brought him Israeli recognition. Until then Israel had absolutely refused to recognize the PLO and Fatah, the predominant party in the PLO, calling it a terrorist organization bent on Israel's destruction, which it surely was.

Various Israeli leaders had tried everything they could to avoid it. Yitzhak Shamir, prime minister twice, the second time from 1986 to 1992, had the not very original idea of developing village leagues, not unlike the good old clan system, where Israel would deal with the heads of each village, showing generosity to those who came to terms with the occupation and severity to those who resisted. The idea was that these tribal chiefs would somehow mold into an alternative to the PLO. They never did, and the idea disappeared into the history books together with Shamir, a short but stocky man, known to have been as stubborn as an ox, with an impressive record as a secret Mossad agent and nicknamed "Mr. Nyet" in diffidence to his habit of saying no to any initiative that may have required Israeli concessions. Shamir was defeated by Rabin, who also desperately tried but failed to find an alternative to Arafat. He tried to develop relations with Faisal Husseini of the old Palestinian Jerusalem family, grandnephew of the mufti of Jerusalem, Mohammed Hajj Amin al-Husseini, a staunch anti-Zionist and ally of Hitler's Germany against the British. Husseini was a founding member of the PLO and the Fatah representative in Jerusalem. To his credit from a Palestinian perspective, he had spent many months in jail and endured interrogation by the Israeli authorities. He was respected and trusted by most Palestinians, even the most radical, and was acceptable as a leader to the Palestinians under Israeli occupation, but only if Arafat said so. Instead Arafat said, "No, no, no," in an interview to the *Jerusalem Report* from his place of exile in Tunis. Humiliated and defeated, forced to leave Beirut with his tail between his legs for Tunisia, the only Arab country that would have him, Arafat still had the power to stifle any Israeli efforts to sideline him. If Husseini had broken ranks and tried to speak for the Palestinians, Arafat could have unleashed a campaign of terror that would have derailed any talks before they started. Arafat's catlike ability to maneuver, to play one off against the other, to be a statesman and a terrorist, an inarticulate stutterer, not an orator, and yet command fealty from isolation and distance was admirable, and something Rabin could not sidestep. He realized that if he was serious about peace, Arafat was his only address.

There is little doubt that Arafat saw Oslo as a first step toward his final goal of getting back all of historic Palestine, especially once the refugees returned. For Rabin, too, Oslo was a stage-by-stage process, but the two sides had exactly opposite goals. Rabin saw the accords as a way of allowing Israel to shed responsibility for the Palestinians, defuse the demographic time bomb, and end the huge outlay in resources that Israel was spending on the occupation and settlements in the territories. As a strategist, he felt that Israel needed to consolidate, to know what it wanted as a nation and what it needed in terms of security. He saw the occupation as debilitating and degrading, the source of erosion in the values of the Israeli army. He also saw it as distracting Israel from dealing with a new existential enemy, Iran, that was beginning to raise its head as a potential nuclear power and was openly dedicated to Israel's destruction.

Rabin did not cook up the Oslo process. It was done almost behind his back by his foreign minister, Shimon Peres, a man he loathed and did not trust. He was more than happy to say so openly and, in case anyone was not listening, to write it for posterity in his autobiography. From Rabin's point of view, if Peres's negotiating team, headed by Uri Savir, a veteran foreign office diplomat, made headway and the talks came to something, he would weigh his options.

He had seen Peres do this dance before, and had seen it crash before. In the mid-1980s, when Yitzhak Shamir headed the country's bipolar national unity government, Peres, then foreign minister as well, after a long and tortuous process of negotiation, met King Hussein secretly at the home of Lord Mishcon in London. The two came to an agreement that would have the Americans call an international conference to resolve Middle East issues. Jordan would regain de facto control of the West Bank; Israel would avoid talking directly to the PLO, and the Palestinian issue would be resolved to the satisfaction of all except the Palestinians themselves. The agreement was signed on April 11, 1987. It was rejected by Shamir, who had no intention of placing Israel's security in the hands of a king who could be toppled at any time, as he would have put it, and give up the Jordan Valley and the West Bank to potential terrorists. He dispatched his defense minister, the amiable former American engineering professor Moshe Arens, to Washington to tell the Americans the agreement was a nonstarter, and so the agreement died. Dead with it was the Jordan option, a solution to the West Bank problem advocated by many, whereby Jordan, a largely Palestinian country, would take the territories back to its control, but with a whole lot of provisos that would act as security guarantees for Israel. By December that year Israel saw its first intifada, or Palestinian uprising, and in July 1988, Jordan renounced all sovereign claims to the West Bank. Israel was stuck with the territories and its million Palestinians for a long time to come, perhaps forever.

I was with Rabin in Washington on the day the intifada broke out, December 8, 1987. I was a fellow at the Washington Institute for Near East Policy and we were hosting him for lunch. Then the cables started to arrive reporting the riots that first started in Gaza, ostensibly because four Palestinians were killed by an Israeli truck driver in an accident in the Jabalia refugee camp. Though there is contention over whether the first intifada was planned, Israeli Intelligence then believed that from his headquarters in Tunis Arafat pushed the button, and a well-organized though seemingly spontaneous but brushfirelike rash of protests broke out all over the territories, including East Jerusalem. The intifada was generally unarmed. The Palestinians, mainly youngsters, used stones, rocks, and even Molotov cocktails against the occupiers. Yet it lasted almost six years and killed 164 Israelis and 2,100 Palestinians, 1,000 of whom were killed by their own people as suspected collaborators. It also finally and unequivocally established the PLO as the only legitimate head of the Palestinian people and ended efforts to seek an alternative. In a way it also reestablished the Green Line, the pre-1967 border that had been obliterated by the years that Israel was now afraid to cross. As the cables came in, Rabin's face got redder and then he uttered in front of many pairs of ears his unfortunate phrase signaling that Israel would crush the riots with force. "We'll break their bones," he infamously spat, setting a tone for the conflict that ultimately caused tremendous harm to Israel's international reputation.

By the time he was elected prime minister for the second time in 1992, Rabin understood that breaking bones did not work, and neither would attempting to sidestep Arafat. In 1991 at the Madrid Conference—hosted by Spain, cosponsored by the United States and the former Soviet Union, and attended by Israel, Syria, Lebanon, Jordan, and the Palestinians—frameworks for future discussions were set up with a view to resolving the conflict regionally. The PLO was not invited, only a Palestinian representative delegation under the Jordanian umbrella delegation, headed by the intelligent and gentlemanly Dr. Haider Abdel-Shafi from Gaza, and including the young and feisty Saeb Erekat, destined later to become the chief Palestinian negotiator with Israel. The intifada and the Gulf War gave birth to Madrid, and in a circumspect way Madrid led to Oslo. Madrid spawned dozens of working committees that had scores of diplomats attending endless discussions for months on end to try to find ways for the countries of the Middle East to live together. As if the plethora of meetings were not enough, think tankers, former government officials, and academics from the parties got together informally, usually under the auspices of a neutral party, and tried to work out solutions to problems.

If Arafat saw Oslo as a way to regain a foothold in Palestine, Rabin saw it as a phased process where each step forward was predicated on the success of the step that preceded it. Arafat would be allowed to come back, initially to Gaza, a Palestinian Authority would be established, territory would be handed over slowly and judiciously to the Palestinians, and eventually, once trust between the sides had been established, the eternal, more complex issues, like Jerusalem, would be dealt with. He saw the process as one in which the Palestinians would undergo a social and national transformation from terrorism to independence and democracy. He thought that the years without confrontation could bring about economic prosperity and cross-border cooperation that in turn might serve as a bulwark against future conflict. What Rabin did not take into account, though he was aware of the hatred around him, was Yigal Amir. No one did. Israel had been so focused on the Palestinians that it never took a deep look at itself. Not that the country was blind to what was happening politically because of Oslo and the handing over of the territories. The papers could not have been more filled with lamentations over the excesses of the Right, which had posters with Rabin dressed up with a kaffiyeh headdress, the type worn by Arafat, plastered all over town and even some doctored to have Rabin dressed in the uniform of the German SS. The secret service had its eye on the crazies from the Jewish underground and their associates, but they were known to have more bark than bite and were certainly not thought to have it in them to assassinate a prime minister. The prime minister's bodyguards at the mass peace event were looking for terrorists with Arab profiles, not a seemingly ordinary Jewish student in a windbreaker. There had been isolated acts of Jewish terrorism over the years, including a hair-raising plot to blow up Temple Mount, but all had been directed against Arabs. And while the rabbis gave somewhat verbal sanction to stone and expunge those who would give up God's land, the secret service did not consider that someone might take them seriously.

The man Amir originally intended to kill, Oslo architect Shimon Peres, must have had the angels watching over him that night, because at the last moment, seeing an opportunity to get

Rabin, Amir changed his mind and directed his bullets toward Rabin instead. Peres automatically succeeded Rabin as prime minister and, though he probably deserved more credit for Oslo than anyone else, would watch it disintegrate as he slipped from power, losing the 1996 election to a young, glib, energetic, and articulate rival, Binyamin Netanyahu, before being shunted to the sidelines by a Netanyahu clone on the Labor side, Ehud Barak, a Rabin protégé whose footprint on Israel would prove much larger than his shoe.

It was not only Netanyahu, however, who beat Peres in the 1996 election. It was Arafat as well. Peres, confident of victory, had called the election to get a mandate to move the peace process forward. This was not what Arafat wanted to hear. With Rabin he had had a careful partner who counted to ten, then twenty, before making a decision. Peres was determined to make a deal, to end the conflict. Arafat, Rabin, and Peres had received the 1995 Nobel Peace Prize; now Peres wanted to make peace his legacy. Arafat, however, had no intention of being pushed into a corner, bullied by President Bill Clinton and Peres into agreeing to end the conflict with Israel in return for 22 percent of historic Palestine without a full return of the refugees. Arafat did not want as his partner a left-wing peacenik who envisioned resolution of the Palestinian issue that left Israel with Jaffa, Haifa, Acre, Ramla, and Lod. Haste was not his game plan. He needed time to establish himself in Palestine, gradually taking over territory, gaining international recognition, being seen to rid the Palestinians of the yoke of Israeli oppression, filling his coffers, and bringing the diverse Palestinian resistance groups under his control. In the meantime, the Palestinian population would grow, the Israelis would continue to debilitate themselves with internal debate and the cost of occupation, and the Palestinians would eventually come out on top. While he grew stronger, the Jews would become weaker. The last thing he needed was Shimon Peres rushing up with an olive branch in his mouth. Like Peres, Arafat, too, had won the Nobel Peace Prize. Unlike Peres, he intended that his legacy be Palestine, not peace.

The true face of Arafat was revealed clearly in a speech he gave in a mosque in Johannesburg, South Africa, shortly after signing the Oslo Accords and shaking Rabin's hand on the White House lawn. He said that the womb of the Palestinian woman was the best weapon the Palestinians had and that what the gun could not achieve, the Palestinian mother would. His message did not resonate then, the country being semi-euphoric over the peace accords with the Palestinians, but to re-read it now is chilling. The essence of his speech was that his Muslim brethren must not be concerned that he had made peace with Israel. On the contrary, this was, he said, the first step on the road to Jerusalem and jihad. As for the agreements themselves: "I am not considering them more than the agreement between our prophet Mohammed and Koresh," he said, not having to add that Koresh had agreed to allow Mohammed to pray in Mecca, but two years later when strong, Mohammed slaughtered the Koresh tribe to the last person and conquered Mecca. That was Arafat's interpretation of the accords at the time, and the Israeli elections that were in the offing were about to bring him closer to his goal.

The elections were scheduled for early May. The polls showed Peres ahead. Despite his endless energy, Netanyahu was making little headway into the Left's core support or even the undecideds.

So in late February Arafat made a strategic decision to go back to his old profession, terrorism, to tip the scales in young Netanyahu's direction, to prove to the Israeli public what they had always suspected about Peres, that he could not be trusted when it came to security. Peres had never served in uniform, despite his close association with Israel's defense establishment all those years as the country's chief procurer and father of its atomic program. Arafat knew that all he had to do was wait for an appropriate moment. They were never long in coming in the volatile Middle East.

Even during Rabin's tenure, there had been a sporadic spate of terrorism, including car bombs and isolated suicide bombings, all of them carried out by Hamas or the Islamic Jihad, an ideal situation for Arafat, who could claim plausible deniability and pledge himself to doing everything he could to stop it. Few could put on a better show than Arafat, his eyes bulging, corpulent lips trembling as he decried terror but did nothing to prevent it.

For months Israel had been closely following a much-wanted terrorist called the "Engineer," who was behind the ordnance so effectively being used by suicide bombers inside Israel. The Israeli security services had told Arafat about their interest in Yahya Ayyash, a twenty-eight-year-old graduate of Bir Zeit University on the West Bank known to be operating out of Gaza, whom they desperately wanted arrested. Arafat promised to see what he could do, which was nothing, and instead waited for the Israelis to take action on their own, which they did, providing Arafat with the trigger he needed. The Shabak, the Israeli secret service, had managed to swap Ayyash's cell phone with an identical one booby-trapped with a bomb, and that was the end of the Engineer, and of Peres's election hopes.

In the first revenge attack on March 3, a suicide bomber killed nineteen when he exploded himself on a crowded bus on Jerusalem's main street, Jaffa Road. On March 4, another suicide bomber exploded himself in the heart of Tel Aviv on Dizengoff Road next to the city's main shopping center, killing thirteen. On March 21, a suicide bomber exploded himself in a Tel Aviv café. One of the injured was a little girl dressed as a baby clown for the festival of Purim, her picture making front-page news the next day. Her mother was killed. My daughter, Maya, was in the café at the time, arguing over her rent with her landlord. Luckily they both escaped, but just as the incident had touched me, so the spate of bombings ripped through Israel, leaving the country furious with Peres and more convinced than ever that Arafat had not changed. Netanyahu did not win the election by much, under half of 1 percent, but that was enough to change the peace dynamic in Israel completely.

SIX

Israeli Politics
in Transition

Netanyahu's first three-year term as prime minister was, by all accounts, a disaster. The task of building up a majority in Israel's 120-person Knesset with only 32 seats would have baffled an experienced politician, let alone one who stormed into power alienating his core political allies, such as Benny Begin, Dan Meridor, and even Ariel Sharon, all key members of the Likud. He had difficulty passing the budget, and soon into his tenure he allowed the opening of a tunnel that ran from under the Temple Mount into the Via Delarosa section of the Old City, nothing important in itself, but explosive given the complexities and sensitivities at the time. Peres had warned him to leave the tunnel alone, though technically Israel had the right to open up the walkway that runs parallel to the Western Wall of the Mount, for archaeological and tourism purposes. Still, it was not wise to do it then, especially in the way in which it was done, at night when it was thought the world was not watching. In the ensuing riots eighty people were killed, and Netanyahu's judgment was called into serious question.

As the months passed, any optimism there had been in Israel began to dissipate. Yet Netanyahu, the man who was elected to guard Israel and ensure the Palestinians got nothing if they gave nothing—"reciprocity," as he called it—finally agreed to carry out an Israeli troop withdrawal from 80 percent of Hebron, as specified by the Oslo Accords, after a tooth-wrenching experience with the Americans and Palestinians, who had become de facto allies against Netanyahu on peace process issues. Suddenly a man who had called the accords a catastrophe was carrying them out; who had called Peres a weakling was giving in; and who had warned against giving the Palestinians control of any more territory was handing over the last Palestinian city on the West Bank to Palestinian control. Netanyahu, who had said Arafat was an arch-terrorist never to be trusted, was shaking the arch-terrorist's hand. Most bizarre, a man whose campaign had declared that Netanyahu was "Good for the Jews" gave away Jewish control over most of Hebron, the holiest Jewish city after Jerusalem, to the Palestinians. This and the Wye River Plantation agreements with Yasser Arafat a year later, in October 1998, essentially recommitting Israel to the Oslo Accords, changed the Israeli Right's perception of itself in a fundamental way for the first time. Instead of being a unified opposition to the Israeli Left with a clear delineation between those who were prepared to give up land for peace and those who were not, now there were deep cracks in the wall and old ideological rifts came to the fore.

With his back to the wall, faced with defections, unable to pass the budget, and desperate to reinvent himself, Netanyahu called an election for May 1999. His opponent, Labor Party wonder boy Ehud Barak, beat him in the personal election by 13 percent, and in the general election the Likud went down to nineteen seats. Shas, the Sephardic ultraorthodox party, received an astounding seventeen seats, making it the third-largest political force in the Knesset, many of its voters defecting from the Likud, having obviously decided to transfer their trust from mortal politicians to God.

Ehud Barak was as disastrous a leader for Labor as Netanyahu had been for Likud. Whatever his intention, he became the politician who killed the peace process, aided by his willing ally in self-destruction, Yasser Arafat. It was truly amazing to me, after years in Israel as a journalist and observer of public affairs, though cynical of politicians, how I could have totally misread someone on the national stage. I thought Ehud Barak was the savior, Rabin's successor, a smart and decisive politician with a deep strategic understanding of the region. He was Israel's most decorated war hero, commander of the country's most elite military unit, former head of military intelligence, chief of staff who was made interior minister by Rabin almost before Barak had hung up his uniform in 1995. Peres made him foreign minister after Rabin's assassination, and immediately after being voted into the Knesset on the Labor list in 1996, Barak started plotting his ascent to power. Working out of his brother-in-law's law office, he set up a civilian version of the "Bor," the military's underground command post in Tel Aviv. Soon, dull lawyers were replaced around the coffee machine by slim, trim, strong, determined, and similarly

71

dressed men in and around their forties. With the same precision they used to plan operations in Sayeret Matkal, where Barak was their commander, they mapped out his conquest with attention to detail, treating it with the same military precision as when they went into the heart of Beirut in April 1973 to avenge the Munich Massacres, dressed as women and arriving in taxis to kill three top PLO commanders in their beds. Funds, later to be found bordering on illegality, were set up, regional headquarters established, and a world-class election strategist hired, in James Carville, the affable political consultant from the American South, who had propelled Bill Clinton into the White House and had a grand time playing political chess with his American colleague Arthur Finkelstein, Netanyahu's key strategist.

Barak won big, not a particularly admirable feat considering Netanyahu's abysmal performance. As prime minister, Barak showed his worth early by pulling the IDF out of Lebanon after a costly eighteen-year presence, and then went on to systematically self-destruct, taking the Israeli Left with him.

It happened because both Clinton and Barak wanted to make a deal with the Palestinians quickly. Barak was a great believer in Oslo, not so much because it gave the Palestinians the beginnings of a state but because, as he put it, the accords separated what he considered a viable Jewish state from the Palestinians. "They over there and us over here" was his favorite slogan at the time, clasping his hands together and moving them first left, then right, as he separated "us" from "them."

That Barak has a character issue is now well known. He is an egomaniac, unable to keep loyal staff around him, manipulative, secretive, and not always entirely honest or straightforward, even by political standards. Like Midas in reverse, he turned gold into stone at every touch. Friends became enemies; supporters, opponents. Within a year of being in power, he saw his coalition dissipate before his eyes, and his own political future heading for the rocks. As winter approached in 1999, his original parliamentary base had shrunk to around thirty from seventy-five, leaving Labor almost entirely isolated.

Ever the strategist, Barak, along with his advisers, decided he needed a new mega event to prove his worth. In December 1999 he attended a summit with the Syrians arranged by the Americans in Shepherdstown outside Washington, D.C., to negotiate a settlement. Optimism ran high that an agreement could be worked out. Instead, Barak was a disaster: he led all sides into believing he had an agreement with the Syrians, then pulled out with cold feet. Conditions could not have been better: the Americans were fully in favor of an agreement and had made countless shuttle trips to try to expedite negotiations; Bashar Assad trusted Barak, a military man like himself, a lot more than he trusted Netanyahu; and previous governments had done most of the groundwork on the form and format of the agreements. One of the Israeli negotiators at the time spread his hands vertically as far as he could to illustrate the pile of documents that had been accrued in the process, from water issues to trade. Israeli troops were out of Lebanon, removing a major source of contention, and Assad's health was failing fast—he would die six months later—which meant this would be the last real chance for peace for a long time to come.

Instead of coming out of it all like a statesman, Barak emerged battered, bruised, and virtually detested by everyone who had anything to do with cooking up the disappointment. But his next act made Shepherdstown and the Syrian fiasco pale in comparison.

Since Rabin's assassination, the Oslo process had effectively stalled. By mid-2000, President Clinton was approaching the end of his second and final term. He had seen Peres, Rabin, and Arafat receive a Nobel Peace Prize and it was generally thought in Israel at the time that the president would very much like one of his own. Barak was drowning in political defections, parties bailing out of his coalition over every possible reason—religion, territory, the economy, and security. His mind was not on the Nobel Prize, but on survival—his own political survival rather than Israel's. For Arafat, the situation could not have been better. While his enemies, the Israelis, threw dirt at one another, he was sitting pretty. He had control of 96 percent of the Palestinian people in the occupied territories and all of Palestine's major cities from which Israeli forces had withdrawn, including most of Hebron. He had at his command at least five security services, all watching one another and reporting exclusively to him. He had control over Palestinian finances and was at the center of a politically supportive bunch of cronies from the days in exile, each of whom had a not insignificant stake in the new Palestinian national companies that had started to emerge. Arafat had played host, red carpets and all, to no less a personage then Clinton himself in 1996, when the president came to shore up what was left of the Oslo peace process after the March suicide bombings in Jerusalem and Tel Aviv.

By contrast, Israeli political parties were fraying and feuding. Fights had broken out, not only between Israel's thirteen or so political parties, but inside them as well. The Right was fractured by territorial concessions, the Left over what Barak should do.

The Palestinians, on the other hand, buoyed by the millennium celebrations in December 1999 that had brought in huge revenues from tourism and investment in infrastructure, were confident, even cocky. Arafat was quite content with the way things were and had no incentive to rock the boat now with peace initiatives that could only present him with challenges he did not want to face or resolve. His goal was all of Palestine, not a third of it, even if it took a hundred years to get there. Anyway, he already had his Nobel Prize.

Barak, however, needed to change the tide against him, and for Clinton, time was running out. He would hand over the White House in six months, and from September would effectively be a lame duck.

Barak determined that he could survive politically only by preempting Israel's elections with a referendum on accepting a peace treaty with the Palestinians. He decided he would call Arafat's bluff and make him an unprecedented offer, one that included the handover of non-Jewish Jerusalem, in return for real, enduring, and meaningful peace.

If Arafat accepted, Barak would hold a referendum to ask the Israeli people directly, not the parliament, to ratify the agreement. As a result, people would reaffirm their belief in his leadership, voters would flock to the Labor Party, his colleagues would revere him again, and Israel's most decorated soldier would be back in the saddle again. Barak reckoned that if Arafat rejected the offer, the country and the world would blame the Palestinians, and the Israeli political consensus would swing behind him, Mr. Security,

Rabin's successor, the best person to navigate Israel through whatever wars developed with the Palestinians as a result of the dissolution of the peace process.

After much secret shuttle diplomacy, Israeli and American diplomats laid the groundwork for a summit in the United States in which Arafat would eventually be offered a package he could not refuse: over 90 percent of the occupied territories for the Palestinian people, a land swap, and all the Old City of Jerusalem other than the Jewish and Armenian Quarters.

On July 5, 2000, President Clinton invited both sides to join him at Camp David for negotiations aimed at bringing the Oslo process to its intended end: peace and the creation of an independent Palestine that would coexist with Israel.

Tremendous pressure was brought on Arafat to attend by the Saudis and whoever else the Americans could muster up, and on July 11, the sides convened at Camp David, the location chosen to echo the 1979 peace talks between Israel and Egypt.

It is customary to say that Arafat was no Sadat, but in one way he was. Sadat said very clearly to Begin in 1979 that peace was predicated on Israel's returning every inch of Egyptian territory. And so it was, down to the very last inch. Arafat had said as clearly that he was prepared for a peace agreement with the Israelis that established an independent Palestine on the eastern side of the 1967 line on the West Bank and in Gaza, but that he could not come to an "end of conflict" agreement that would legitimize Israel's continued presence on two-thirds of historic Palestinian land and without the refugees' being able to return to their historic homes. These two cardinal pillars of Arafat's philosophy were known to all the parties at Camp David.

Prior to the talks, advisers, including some of my colleagues, emphasized this very point to Barak: he cannot give you "end of conflict"; go for a simple peace agreement that leaves some core issues open. It would give the Israelis and the Palestinians time to work together, to open up trade and a whole new world. Peace would evolve into an end to the conflict if allowed to take its own course. It was the route Rabin would have taken. Barak was told not to go in like a bull in a china shop but to be aware of the meaning of the semantic ideological borders the Palestinians wouldn't cross. Peace would be an admirable outcome. Also, he was told, don't deal with all the final status issues now, pushing Arafat into a corner. With the Egyptians, a peace agreement was signed at Camp David and only sixteen months later the details were settled. Barak was advised to omit Jerusalem, the Temple Mount, and refugees. Put them into committee. A final deal would be made with the next, post-Arafat generation of Palestinian leaders, which would be less ideological and more pragmatic. Having spent their lives under Israeli occupation, they knew that six million Jews were not going anywhere. Make bold steps, Barak was told, but don't walk over the edge.

Barak being Barak listened but did not hear. At Camp David he and Clinton spent almost two weeks, July 11 to 24, trying to get Arafat to bend, which, of course, he would not do. Clinton could not grasp that for Arafat, Palestine included every inch.

Arafat also believed the goal would ultimately be attainable only if the Palestinian question was kept alive, not partially resolved. He was all for peace—but one that allowed the Palestinians to continue to consolidate while the Jews became weaker as they fought one another. Ending the conflict with Israel would be a dam in the way of the demographic flood and a fire extinguisher to the flames of the Palestinian cause. There was no way Arafat could agree.

Yet Barak could agree to nothing less. The sides were on a collision course that would inevitably deal yet another blow to the peace process. Arafat came out of the summit belittled by Clinton and reviled by the pro-Western Arabs and his European donors, who thought he had missed a historic opportunity on behalf of the Palestinian people.

Barak initially looked stupid, having made concessions that no Israeli had thought even vaguely possible before the summit while claiming that he had unmasked Arafat and shown the world that Israel did not have a true partner in peace. President Clinton was frustrated, even furious that his legacy would be perceived as one of failure in the Middle East. The failure of Camp David caused new ruptures in Israeli politics, including the return to center stage of Menachem Begin's political nemesis, Ariel Sharon. In the Palestinian territories the young generation was proud that Arafat had managed to resist massive pressure, but its members were left asking themselves what type of future they faced since Arafat had rejected everything they had been taught to believe they were fighting for: an independent Palestine with Jerusalem as its capital, recognized by the whole world, and living in peace was a dream. Now it had been blown away by their leader. The "Young Guard," as they were called, had sent emissaries and messages to Arafat to work out a deal at Camp David, but to no avail. Before they could articulate their resentment, Arafat would push the destruct button again, this time with a massive intifada, an all-out war against the Jewish state, intended not to bring its de-

mise, but to initiate a long-haul war of attrition that would significantly weaken Israel's morale, economically and in terms of
its own sense of security. It would also distract Palestinian criticism from Arafat's own leadership. There is nothing like a good
war to foster internal unity. What Arafat needed was an excuse,
a trigger.

It was provided by Ariel Sharon, the man who had overseen
Arafat's humiliating exile from Beirut eighteen years before.
Sharon was running for leadership of the Likud, a position from
which he would go on to win the general election. His obvious
political tactic was to discredit Oslo, vilify Arafat, and repeat ad
nauseam that he would never divide Jerusalem. To prove it, he
decided to visit Temple Mount on September 28, with a contingent of hundreds of security men and journalists in tow, as if to
stake his claim to Haram al-Sharif, the third-holiest site of Islam.
The visit sparked a series of violent riots that in a few days left
some fifty Palestinians dead, including some who had gone to the
Mount to pray on the Friday following the Sharon visit, and hundreds injured. The Second Intifada had begun.

There have been long discussions about whether the Sharon
visit sparked the intifada and whether Arafat had planned it. The
head of Israeli military intelligence at the time was adamant that
the riots were spontaneous and that Arafat was "riding the tiger,"
while his colleague over at General Security Services insisted
that there was no tiger and that Arafat was running the show. It
now seems that the intifada started spontaneously but was soon
channeled by Arafat to his advantage. Arafat always said that
one of the great advantages the Palestinians had over the Israelis
was that the Palestinians had patience and steadfastness, *sumud*,

the ability to suffer, while the Jews were weak and fickle, needed everything done quickly, and could not take punishment. Time, he firmly believed, was on Palestine's side and war was what he needed to gain time.

The Second Intifada was different from Israel's other wars, and I have seen them all since 1967. It was madness. There were no rules of engagement, no Geneva Conventions, no uniformed or visible enemy, and no defined battlefield. After four years, when Arafat finally died, 5,500 Palestinians and 1,100 Israelis had died. The Palestinians deployed to devastating effect their suicide bombers. Able to reach almost any target, in all weather, day or night, and explode at will, the suicide bombers hit Israel where it hurt most—at or near homes, schools, neighborhoods, and cafés.

From October 2000 on, for four long and terrible years, you and your family and friends were not safe in a bus or in the mall, not going to school or attending a birthday party. Fear was everywhere. Tourism ceased. Restaurants went broke. Hotels closed entire floors. If you drew up next to a bus at a red light, you prayed for the light to change as quickly as possible. You bought your children cell phones so you knew where they were at all times. In some cases entire families were wiped out, three generations in one attack, something that had not happened since the Holocaust. Security guards were placed in the front of all businesses and public places. The property market dried up. Construction stopped.

Unemployment rose. It was a time of despair and darkness, of wondering what type of country we were bringing our children up in and deeply questioning what type of future they would have. Peace no longer seemed possible; it was unimaginable that we could live with these "savages" who murdered innocent civilians in cold blood and hated us so much that they were prepared to allow their children to take part in the insanity. What future was there for either side?

Arafat was not behind all of the suicide bombings. Most of them were carried out by Hamas, the Islamic fundamentalist arm of the Palestinian armed struggle at the time. But the bombings suited Arafat's purpose. It was his assessment that a protracted war against the Israeli heartland, where women and children and not just soldiers were being killed, would break the country's spirit.

If he could cripple the economy, many of the new immigrants who had recently arrived from the former Soviet Union whose ties to Israel were tenuous at best would pack up and leave, as would others who had an alternative to the mayhem and hell he was creating. Arafat capitalized on years of suffering by the Palestinians, preached to them about Palestinian strength and Israeli weakness, and urged them to read the panicky headlines and commentaries in the Israeli press. It was only a matter of time, he promised, before the Jews would flee and Palestinian historic rights would be restored. He did not, however, fully take Ariel Sharon into account. As expected, Sharon won the May election. Never before had so few people, some 64 percent, turned out to vote. There was little enthusiasm for Sharon, but even those who could not bring themselves to vote for him admitted that given the security situation, he was the best candidate for the job. Arafat had mauled Israel's young leaders—Netanyahu and Barak—as if they were cubs. It was time for experience. Israel needed a bastard of its own. In the minds of many, the Arabs were getting the Israeli leadership they deserved.

Ehud Barak's legacy, however, was not Sharon. It was the death of the Israeli Left that for years had been advocating "land for peace," relinquishing the territories conquered in the 1967 war and a return to the Green Line in exchange for the creation of an independent Palestinian state that would live in peace with Israel.

The failure at Camp David and the ensuing violence were seen by both the Israeli Left and the Israeli Right as a total renunciation of the concept that peace was possible if Israel returned to the 1967 borders. Barak had offered Arafat a deal considered by all to be substantial, fair, and beyond what any other Israeli had offered in the past. Still, the Palestinians wanted it all.

But the intifada did not break Israel as Arafat had imagined and had promised his would-be martyrs. The mass exodus never happened. Instead, the ultraorthodox, never an integral part of the modern democratic secular Jewish state, headed the paramedic services, collected body parts, visited bereaved families and the injured, took in orphaned children, and became, for the first time, victims and participants in Israel's wars. Instead of packing their bags and leaving, those who came from the former Soviet Union became fully part of the country. The dead now were not only Eli and Avi but also Leonid and Larissa.

These were people who were also sick and tired of being hassled by others and being told what to do and how to do it because they were Jewish. They had put up with latent and blatant anti-Semitism for years. They were in no mood to tolerate more, and had no intention of moving yet again. Israel was their home. As a community, they had issues with the rabbinate and the government over absorption, but instead of running away they became a powerful force on the Israeli Right, their newspapers, commentators, and politicians holding some of the most extreme nationalist positions in Israeli politics. This aside, their addition to Israeli society helped change the demographic balance against the Arabs and added yet another layer to Israel's survivability, while greatly enriching Israel culturally, pluralistically, and educationally, given the high proportion of academics, specifically in mathematics and the sciences, who came.

 SEVEN

The Red Light

At first Ariel Sharon's position was that constraint was strength: there was no need to rush back into the territories after every suicide bombing. Other surgical means were available that would not drag Israeli troops back into the occupied towns of the West Bank and the refugee camps, actions that would cost Israeli soldiers their lives. Every corner and building would be booby-trapped. Suicide bombers would be lurking in the shadows. The international media, together with international public opinion, would take another swipe at the Israeli Goliath, as tanks rumbled through towns and civilians fled for their lives. Sharon looked instead at targeted assassination, deepening the intelligence effort in the territories, reprisals directly against the PA and Arafat, preemptive arrests, liberal use of the Emergency Regulations, house demolitions, banishments, and curfews. But Sharon's patience and that of the country ended on the night of March 27,

2002, when twenty-five-year-old Abdel-Bassat Odeh from the West Bank city of Tulkarem walked into the dining room of the Park Hotel in Netanya where he worked as a waiter and blew himself to bits. He was dressed as a woman at the time. Of the 250 guests, 30 were killed and 140 injured, almost all of them elderly people who had come to the hotel for Passover seder because they had nowhere else to go.

It was one of those moments one does not forget. In Jerusalem we were sitting down at the beautifully laid table for the traditional four glasses of wine, shrieks from the children in the background arguing over what presents they were going to extract from their parents for returning the *afikomen*, when the phone rang. It was for Martin Indyk, a dear friend and then the American ambassador to Israel. He returned, his face ashen. We had lived with death and terror for almost two years. My son Gavriel, then nine, passed by a bus just minutes after it had been bombed, on the way to school with his mom one Friday morning at the Patt Junction. He heard the sirens of the ambulances and police cars, saw the smoke, heard the screams and cries of the wounded, and very innocently turned to Isabel and asked, "Are we in the Holocaust, Mommy?" And Lev, his little brother, had just missed seeing a suicide bomber explode while he was on his way to kindergarten at Beit Shmuel near the Hebrew Union College. The bomber's head was hanging from a balcony of the David Citadel Hotel, and an unexploded grenade landed in the playground of Lev's kindergarten, just over the wall.

As ambassador, Indyk had also been through a lot. It was on his watch that the March 1996 explosions took place, and he was the American ambassador here at the time of Rabin's assassination. My wife, Isabel, was a hardened journalist. But the Park Hotel bombing shocked us all. It was horrendous. The symbolism of Jews, old Jews, being slaughtered on the festival of freedom, like sheep, pushed that "never again" button in many. Sharon could no longer preach restraint. The die had been cast. It was time to change the rules of the game—again. Though there had recently been a Saudi initiative and a promising Arab peace conference in Beirut, in truth I had never felt further from peace in Israel. No matter what I voted, I felt, it would make no difference. Things had lost all proportion, all rationality.

Bringing suicide bombing under control required a period of intense military action, including the re-invasion of the West Bank by Israeli forces in the biggest operation there since 1967. In a defensive measure, Sharon also ordered a security barrier erected between Israel and troublesome areas of the West Bank. Very quickly Israel had retaken all the major towns, and even the refugee camps where dire casualties had been predicted for Israel but did not materialize. Before long, through mass arrests, including some of the top Fatah leadership, the occupation was back, perhaps with greater force than before. Many of those now in the infantry units patrolling the territories were truculent Russians, whose welcome to Israel had been tempered by the intifada, and whose attitudes toward Arabs had been affected in turn.

Key to quelling the intifada was virtually locking up Arafat in his office, situated in his semi-destroyed headquarters with dubious plumbing and generally unsanitary conditions in an old British fort in Ramallah, called the Mukata. It was there that Arafat eventually would disintegrate into sickness, isolated, cut off from his people, and unable to function. It was a crueler punishment than the exile from Beirut with 2,000 loyalists to Tunis in 1982 and, one suspects, a punishment that Sharon enjoyed every minute administering. He had not only wiped the smile off the Cheshire cat but taken his cream away as well. As pictures and reports emerged from the Mukata, it was clear Arafat's suffering was immense. He must have known his dream had died and that he would remain a prisoner in his own land, doomed to a slow and lonely death from causes never made public and locked forever in the secret archives of the military hospital in Paris where he breathed his last breath.

For Sharon quelling the intifada was a military task, not dissimilar to the one he had conducted as a paratroop officer in Gaza thirty-five years before. His most significant legacy, however, was his decision to unilaterally pull out of Gaza, ending Israel's military presence there and uprooting all twenty-one settlements and 8,500 settlers in the process. It was an act of political bravery with lasting consequences. He did so in defiance of his party. Binyamin Netanyahu—the same man who gave up Hebron—was his main critic. Sharon also defied his generals, sacking Chief of Staff Moshe "Bogie" Ya'alon, who opposed the withdrawal, and appointing the more compliant air force commander Dan Halutz to the most powerful position in the Israeli armed forces, if not in Israel, the first pilot to head the army.

Netanyahu predicted that the Gaza withdrawal would bring rockets on the Israeli south in its wake. He was right. He said it would lead to a Hamas takeover and the radicalization of the Strip, and he was right again. Sharon weighed the cost of keeping 8,500 Jews in Gaza, requiring a division permanently stationed there, against the removal of more than a million Palestinians and decided that Israel was better served by having to tolerate a few rockets a year on Sderot and Ashkelon. The move allowed him to concentrate Israel's security efforts on the West Bank, and effectively cut off Hamas in Gaza from the West Bank. The disengagement also signaled to the Palestinians that the days of their dictating Israel's national agenda were over.

Getting out of Gaza was good for Israel, and Sharon was not going to wait for the Palestinians to come to some agreement that would make it possible. He believed, correctly, that the Palestinians wanted Israel to keep Gaza for the very same reasons Sharon wanted to get rid of it. "We are like a cancer for you," a Gaza acquaintance, a journalist, once sadly told me over dinner. "If I were you I would cut it off."

Sharon was surgical. With clockwork efficiency and a public diplomacy machine the likes of which had never been seen in Israel before, the operation was carried out with "determination and compassion," in the terminology of the IDF, in the last two weeks of August 2005. So efficient was the enforced exodus that even the dead in the small Jewish cemetery were exhumed and transported back to Israel. By the early morning of August 30, when the last Jewish soldier out of there locked the gate, almost 10,000 people had been evicted, the settlers having been joined by outside supporters, and every home and structure built by the Jews, other than five synagogues left standing, was razed to the ground. Nothing but rubble remained of Israel's thirty-five-year sojourn in Gaza, started by the Labor government with much fanfare in the 1970s and destroyed by the Likud's Ariel Sharon, the main architect of Israel's settlement policies for decades and a person whose basic ideology had been to not give up one inch.

A vast majority of the Israeli public, as high as 80 percent in some polls, supported Sharon, but a deep schism developed. As the Gaza evacuation became imminent, so the West Bank settlers started a major campaign against the move, mobilizing the considerable resources they had at their disposal to organize mass demonstrations and publicity campaigns against it. With them stood Netanyahu, a good portion of the Likud's right wing, and the national religious and ultraorthodox parties, all of whom saw this as the first step in giving up Eretz Yisrael, the beginning of the end for the settlement movement's almost unhindered growth until then. With the twenty-one settlements in Gaza, Sharon also decided to close down and destroy four Israeli settlements in the northern West Bank on the pretext that they were isolated. There was a message in the deed, however, and it was well understood. For a long time now, since assuming his role as prime minister, Sharon had said that Israel could no longer live as a conqueror and survive as a democracy, that it had to consolidate, and that it could no longer go on supporting distant communities that were tactical and strategic liabilities.

The settler response came mainly from young teens, male and female students in the Zionist Orthodox yeshiva system that, unlike the yeshivas of the ultraorthodox, had love of land, defense of country, and willingness to serve at the heart of their value system. They were second- and third-generation settlers, men and boys who wore white shirts with short sleeves, blue jeans, and sandals on Shabbat eve no matter the weather, and feisty young women who wore pants under their skirts, spent their summer vacations establishing illegal hilltop settlements, and took great pride in giving soldiers and police a hard time when they were evacuated. For these kids the Gaza evacuation, coming at the same time as the July holidays, was almost like summer camp: they formed a human chain from Jerusalem to Gaza, all wearing orange shirts, the color being declared the "official color" of the anti-withdrawal protest movement, and held all-night sing-alongs by campfires, plotting the next day's activities, how best to confound the authorities and the police and get the camera's eye, perhaps the most important part of the exercise. Central highways were blocked, the entrance to cities made impassable by crowds of protestors, and there were even rumblings within the armed forces about having to go through with an evacuation they assumed would be violent.

In the end the disengagement was achieved without serious resistance. The evacuees were treated very poorly, though. Many live in temporary homes to this day, and the incidence of alcoholism and drug abuse among the youngsters is much higher than the national norm. Those who took the government's early compensation offers did quite well. Those who did not and stayed put in Gaza until the last minute, who believed that the day would never come, got very little. Holding on to their homes, they made no preparations to leave and were dragged onto the buses, taking with them only what they could carry. Their treatment resonated deeply within the wider settler community, who saw it as a portent of what they themselves could face one day.

The real significance lay in the fact that two of Israel's greatest warriors, Sharon and Ehud Barak, foremost strategists and acknowledged security experts, had both come to the same conclusion from two different spectrums of the political scale: it was vital for Israel's future that the territories be returned, a Palestinian entity established, with the understanding that "we" live here, and "they" live there. The mainstream Labor and Likud view overlapped; experienced heads had come to a common view. This had serious unforeseen consequences: opponents of the removal of the settlements, finding no support for their view in the center, drifted to the extreme fringes, empowering radical parties that were marginal beforehand.

The intifada had led Israel to unilateralism, on the basis that victory over the Palestinians was impossible and that the continuation of the status quo would ultimately lead to Israel's destruction, either through internecine conflict over the future of the territories or through escalating violence. From being marginal and peripheral to the core Middle East strategic dimension, helpless and hapless victims, the Palestinians had become a strategic factor, capable of posing an existential threat to Israel with demography and terror as their weapons.

But some believed otherwise. The settlement movement knew that its future was becoming uncertain. Sharon had signed an agreement with the Bush administration called "The Roadmap," which contained a provision that Sharon commit to taking down twenty-two so-called illegal outposts, not that the rest of them were recognized as legal, as a gesture of goodwill and seriousness toward resolving the conflict.

For the religious-Zionist community, the core of ideological settlers on the West Bank, the Gaza settlements had been one thing. Even the most radical or romantic settler would have a hard sell claiming that Gaza was God-given or holy. The area is not part of Israel's biblical narrative at all, other than as the home of the Philistines and some brief mention of Samson bringing down the pillars there, an act of biblical destruction, hardly nation-building. The West Bank—Judea and Samaria—however, was totally different. For all Jews but particularly the religious, it is at the heart of Israel's story, the cord that ties the people to the land. This is what made Israel different from the Jewish state Theodor Herzl briefly considered establishing in Uganda. Judea and Samaria, Schem (Nablus) and Hebron, Sabastia and Beit El, and, of course, Jerusalem, are there, deep in the biblical narrative. This has always been Israel, the touchstone through the dispersions and hell the Jewish people have been through over the centuries. It was this tangible connection to a defined "home to be reached when the storm has passed" that kept the Jews alive as a people when other civilizations disappeared into the folds of history. The fires of the Holocaust, redemption, and return to the land were in the prophecies. In the view of the ideological settlers, no mortal Israeli politician had the right to give away what God had promised and penned on parchment for posterity in the Bible.

The settlers knew Sharon. He had been their biggest ally. "The Bulldozer" had taught them the system: first a watchtower, then a fence, a water tank, a few tents and caravans, an access road, generator-supplied electricity, a small military detachment, and bingo, a new Jewish settlement in the holy land.

Now Sharon had turned his bulldozer on them and for the first time the settlers felt there was a real chance that their life's work was in jeopardy. They were desperate, reaching for any assistance they could find. On one bizarre occasion, fresh back from a trip to Chicago, hardly had I unpacked my bag when I received an urgent call from the defense ministry, even though it had been years since I had been a military reporter. The late-night call was from an acquaintance, a lovely, warm, and cuddly chap who wore sandals no matter the weather and who was also a stalwart of the settlement movement. For some months he had been serving as the ministerial adviser on settlement affairs in the ministry of defense. Now he needed to speak to me at once. On arrival at the gates to the impressive new ministry building on Kaplan Street in Tel Aviv, a gate I have passed a thousand times, always with some degree of difficulty as a journalist, I was greeted by two young female soldiers who whisked me through the gate procedures as if I were some dignitary, or at least chief of some staff. They affably led me through the second, third, and fourth set of security barriers, into an express elevator, and into the first of two huge offices occupied by my acquaintance. There must have been a dozen or so soldiers, all young, darting around in every direction, maps with arrows in different colors on the walls. The office had all the trappings of a military headquarters. My acquaintance and I shook hands and over coffee chatted briefly about the cold weather in the south Hebron area where he lived. Then we got down to business. A stick was thrust at one of the aerial photographs on the wall showing the undulating hills of the central and northern West Bank. On the tip of a hill above a Palestinian village called Sinjil and the Jewish settlement of Shiloh was one of the illegal outposts doomed for destruction under the "Roadmap" agreements Sharon had reached with the Americans. He pointed at the few caravans, water tower, and access road on the hilltop overlooking what must have been breathtaking scenery, and said, "The Mishkan, Holy Ark, stood here for seven years. It is a holy place. It is inconceivable, almost blasphemous, that Israel would consider destroying it. You know the American ambassador, Daniel Kurtzer," he said. "Tell him we can remove some of the outposts; we all know how to get things done without doing them, but this one has to stay. It has strategic value as well. And then, the endgame: you tell him, Hirsh, that if the ambassador agrees to leave this one off the list, we will call it after him— Mitzpeh Daniel." It was a simply preposterous idea. Slowly I realized that I was sitting opposite a totally sincere and innocent person who had done everything he could to save at least one of the outposts destined to be taken down.

One could be fooled by the innocent but sincere request from my acquaintance into thinking that there was something naive and spacey about the settlers, that they are a starry-eyed, messianic bunch with no hold on reality. Nothing could be further from the truth. Never in the history of Israeli politics have a group been more successful, more influential and politically savvy than the settler community. Most of the founders are graduates of the Bnei Akiva religious Zionist youth movement and disciples of the school of the Rav Kook, which saw the conquest of the territories in 1967 as a deliverance from God. They were unstoppable in their march to tie Judea and Samaria to Israel forever—and the Golan and Gaza, if they could be kept in the package. Masters of manipulation, muscle, influence, and God's intentions, they managed to have every single Israeli government since the early 1970s support their settlement binge, sometimes for strategic reasons, other times for historical and emotional ones. By 2005 they were the de facto masters of the land, carrying out their every whim and wish by creating new facts on the ground while the bureaucrats turned a convenient blind eye to the steady encroachment on West Bank Palestinian lands and, as a result, an ever-intrusive presence in the Palestinians' lives. With the settlers came roadblocks and often entire highways closed to non-Israeli traffic, depending on security circumstances. There were then some 270,000 settlers, excluding those in East Jerusalem, living on 121 settlements on the West Bank. They were in the east, west, north, south, and center, joined by roads, protected by the army, with an excellent network of schools designed to create more settlers, and social services with the same goal in mind. The model seemed to be working flawlessly until Sharon came along. The man who uprooted Israel from Gaza was also the man who had once told the youngsters of the settler movement to "grab the hilltops of the West Bank." The problem is they never forgot.

* * *

Sukkoth, the feast of tabernacles, is always a joyous time in Israel, whether secular or religious. It is a time when children make decorations for the traditional booths, the sukkah, with roofs that allow one to see the stars at night, a time to thank God for the bounty, a time when crops are sown and gathered, and when the smell of the first rains come after Israel's long, hot summer. It is a time of celebration when marketplaces bustle with vendors selling palm branches and *etrogim*, citrons, that accompany prayers over the seven-day holiday, and when usually dour Jerusalem comes to life as tens of thousands of pilgrims flood in, Sukkoth being one of the three annual pilgrimage festivals to Jerusalem.

For years now we have been going to the home of Uncle Ivor and his wonderful family for the first night, pleased to be in a traditional atmosphere with people we really like. It would be hard to find a more stalwart, salt-of-the-earth family in Israel. Ivor held a sensitive civil service job for years and Miryam's parents were of the founding generation that took in orphans and built sterling educational institutions. Their children, each and every one of them, could not be more decent, and it is as if the grandchildren literally fell off the same tree.

Each year the ritual is very similar: Food is brought down from a modest first-floor apartment in one of Jerusalem's older and more staid neighborhoods, to the sukkah in the garden, to which an electric cord has been extended and two bulbs attached. A long, narrow table with benches and folding chairs with a spotless white cloth has been set inside, paper plates and plastic cutlery neatly arranged. There are two challot and a pot of honey, and a pitcher of water and a bucket to wash one's hands and say the traditional blessings. And on the walls, kept from one year to the next, the best of the children's sukkah decorations in nylon protective coverings.

In 2006, something was different. And so it has been each year since. The songs were the same, as were the blessings and decorations, but prominent on the wall, where usually the Israeli flag was pinned proudly, was a similar flag, but with an orange background instead of white, and the two parallel stripes of the flag and of the Star of David in its center, black instead of blue. Orange was the color of the anti-disengagement movement of the year before, and black in mourning for the uprooted settlements of Gaza. The dislocation of the national flag was a clear sign that if the settlement issue were taken further, a lasting internal rift might develop. Here, in this sukkah, on one of the most festive occasions of all, received with white shirts and subtle spices, goodwill and hope, in the home of some of the worthiest people I know, had appeared a flag of mourning for the Jewish state.

 EIGHT

The Ball
of Thorns

If Israel wants to survive internally and not destroy itself from within, any peace agreement with the Palestinians has to take Uncle Ivor into account. Israel cannot afford to lose people like him. Though torn between Torah and democracy, they constitute the backbone of modern Israel, the last real pioneers, the bridge between religion and state. In 2011 the national religious Zionists make up over 30 percent of the officers' corps of the ground forces of the Israeli army. These youngsters have grown up believing in the Torah as taught by their rabbis, religion with a deep nationalist twist to it. They are also third-generation settlers who genuinely have no idea where the Green Line, the 1967 boundary, was, nor do they accept it. By the time they got into the army, Jerusalem had been united under Israeli rule for over forty years, more than twice their own lifetimes, and for them the reunification of the city was no less miraculous and God-given than the founding of the modern Zionist state. These youngsters have grown up in a bubble. Settler children all attend the same schools with the same agenda and syllabus, boys and girls apart. What they read and hear is tightly controlled, the radio tuned to Arutz Sheva, Channel Seven, the settler channel, and if there is a newspaper in the house it will be *Makor Rishon*, the right-wing nationalist paper, or, for the more daring, *Ma'ariv*, the less sensational and more staid of Israel's daily papers. The settlers' lives revolve around the community, study and serving the country in one way or another. When I was in the army oh so many years ago, *kippot*, skullcaps, were few and far between, especially in combat units. There was, to my memory, one religious helicopter pilot. The transformation has been profound. Go to the officers' training course near Mitzpeh Rimon in the Negev and count the number of religious settler cadets; attend a pilot graduation class or spend a few hours with Sayeret Matkal, Israel's foremost reconnaissance unit trained to operate behind enemy lines, and the predominance of religious fighters is patently obvious. What the kibbutzim were to Israel in the first fifty years of the state, serving in totally disproportionate numbers in key military units, the graduates of the national religious movement have now become. The difference is that officers from the kibbutz movement were never placed in the same dilemma as officers from the settlement movement: during the Gaza evacuation, some of the settlers were ordered to throw their grandparents out of their homes.

By the end of 2010 some 330,000 Jews lived on the West Bank in what is to be Palestine. An additional 200,000 were living in

Jewish neighborhoods in contested East Jerusalem. While the world has always focused on the Palestinian refugees' demand for a right of return in the context of a peace agreement, a solution has to be found for the situation of the settlers in any peace agreement. To a large degree, the issue of the Palestinian right of return is one of principle. With few of the 1948 refugees still alive, and their families long settled in other countries, not even the Palestinians expect masses of people to be knocking on Israel's door and asking for admission. But the settler problem is young and contentious. At the core are the 80,000 or so settlers who live outside settlement blocs contiguous to the Israeli border, which would probably remain in Israel under any peace plan in return for an approximate land swap elsewhere, and beyond the security barrier that is assumed to be the future border between Israel and the Palestinian state. Some of these 80,000 could be lured to leave their homes on the West Bank and return to Israel with generous grants and other economic incentives, but many of them are hardcore, ideological settlers who, at the same time, are an integral part of modern Israel. Whatever agreement is eventually reached, they have to be factored in. The Palestinians have to realize that Israel cannot be expected to tear itself to pieces for the sake of peace. Peace should mean that 50,000 or so Jews could live in Palestine as Israeli citizens, voting in Israeli elections but paying their local taxes to the Palestinian Authority, which would in turn guarantee the safety and security of those settlers who chose to remain in Palestine, and would cooperate fully with the Israeli security services to ensure that this was the case.

The settlers in turn would have to live as good neighbors and control their violent and fanatic elements, a small minority. The details would need to be teased out, but the principle is clear: any future agreement with the Palestinians must allow Jews who want to remain in what they consider biblical Judea and Samaria to do so. There are, after all, over a million Palestinians living and prospering in Israel. So why should not 50,000 Jews or so thrive among over two million Arabs?

It is a question, not only of Jews living among Palestinians, but also of how the Palestinians plan to live among themselves. In 2007 the Palestinians became a people divided between the West Bank and Gaza. Gaza was in the hands of Hamas, a militant, supported, Islamic-fundamentalist faction that won parliamentary elections in 2006, then wrested control of the coastal enclave from the Palestinian Authority in 2007, while the Authority continued to maintain control over the West Bank. The Fatah-dominated PA and Hamas hated each other with a passion that only fratricide can generate, and repeated attempts by outside parties at conciliation had failed. In the takeover of Gaza, Hamas showed no mercy, throwing Fatah loyalists off the tallest building in the Strip and having gangs of hooligans kill others, including so-called collaborators with Israel, who were shot without trial. Hamas went on to control Gaza with an iron hand, with morality patrols to make sure there was no public entertainment, including women smoking narghiles in cafés, no cinemas, and no Internet cafés, or women bathing on the beaches, the only forms of relaxation available in the claustrophobic reality of Gaza. Summer camps—including those run by UNWRA, the UN relief agency—that did not teach Islamic studies and conform to Hamas's strict syllabus were burned. Under the Israeli-led economic blockade, Gaza became a place of high unemployment, with no industry, no port despite its Mediterranean coastline, no functioning airport, cut off by Egypt to the south and Israel to the west and north. Mainly it became a place of no hope. Hamas's leadership in Damascus called the shots, far away from the misery of daily life in Gaza. According to polling done by Dr. Khalil Shikaki's Ramallah-based Palestine Center for Policy and Survey Research, released in March 2011, two-thirds of the general population of Gaza and 75 percent of the youth wanted regime change and conciliation with the West Bank and the Palestinian Authority. Hamas is not impervious to these demands and pays lip service to them from time to time. When the steam rises, Hamas yields and signs a reconciliation agreement with Fatah, the terms only to be forgotten once the ink has dried and the cameras are packed away. Hamas is deeply ideological and will not recognize Israel's right to exist. On that it has been unbending. It also looks as if the group's hold on Gaza, a tiny speck of land fifty kilometers long and fifteen to twenty kilometers wide, will be in place for a long time to come. Gaza's isolation from the outside world and its small size make it easy to control. Although Hamas has always opposed peace with Israel and developed suicide bombing and crude rocket manufacturing into a fine art, it is prepared for a ten- to fifteen-year *hudna*, or truce, with Israel with an option for an extension, during which the Palestinians will have more babies. Meanwhile, hedonistic Israel will melt into the global village and Palestine will be liberated forever.

The *hudna* serves a practical function as well as a strategic one: once Hamas was running Gaza, it had to provide for the people there or face insurrection. For this it needed to have more or less normal relations with Israel that would allow an inflow and export of goods.

Whether Hamas Damascus or the Iranians would accept a *hudna* is another story and another indication of the dichotomy between those living in Gaza and the outside command. Iran and Hamas Damascus need to keep the conflict alive, sometimes on a low burner but alight and ready to flare up. Hamas Gaza wants an Islamic state, but one with a modicum of normalcy and not a situation where men between eighteen and thirty are being paid through Hamas benevolent funds not to work and graduates are unable to either find jobs or leave the Strip for somewhere else. Hamas has to make the prison livable and open its borders to the outside, and therein lies a possible framework for understanding between Hamas in Gaza and Israel. That is why Hamas Damascus and Iran are so opposed to any normalcy at all. They want *shahids*, martyrs, to be turned on and off at will, and for that the people have to be kept miserable. How long Gazans will put up with this is another question, but whatever the answer, Israel has to move ahead with peace without Gaza. It can no longer allow Iran and Damascus to dictate its future. It has to move on. There is a potential partner on the West Bank, and that is where Israel has to invest its energies.

If Gaza wants conflict, so be it. For Israel, frankly, it is more of a public relations problem than a military one at this stage. Virtually no weapons systems supplied to Hamas will outmatch the Israeli military and, as with Hezbollah, the more sophisticated the weapons, the easier they are for Israel to destroy. Home-made Kassam rockets, launched from tubes with clockwork timers, can cross the border with impunity. But once electronic, magnetic, radar, or heat signatures are involved, Israel is well equipped to deal with the problem, as was so dramatically demonstrated by Iron Dome in early 2011.

While Gaza has languished under the blockade, on the West Bank there has been economic growth, strong contacts with the pro-Western Arab world, Europe, and the United States. There is fiscal and governmental transparency, a strong tourism industry that brings in over a million tourists a year to the West Bank conditional on stability. The Palestinian Authority has made great strides in instituting civil rule and authority. Cities like Jenin and Nablus, which until a few years ago were controlled by armed gangs taking advantage of the chaos caused by the intifada, are orderly, clean, and increasingly prosperous and proudly showing themselves off to the international press. Police trained by the Europeans, and security forces by an American-funded program, are present all over the place and, unlike Gaza, are welcomed by the general public and seen to be keeping law and order. Dr. Saeb Erekat, the chief Palestinian negotiator, told me in the autumn of 2010, while driving to a conference together, that the youngsters of the best Palestinian families were going into the security forces, seeing themselves as the harbingers of a Palestinian state to be proud of. On a recent trip to Ramallah, the results of the European and American efforts were apparent everywhere, investment obviously flowing into the place, with dozens of cranes dotting the landscape. The streets were clean, the shops buzzing, traffic flowing, and neat and courteous policemen everywhere. The atmosphere was unthreatening. There was a strong sense that the West Bank Palestinians wanted to get on with their lives, that they had made their point with two intifadas, that the world—including Israel—favored an independent Palestinian state, and that they could not wait forever for the Palestinians in Gaza to shed the yoke of Hamas to move forward. This was not a question of divide and rule, as some may suspect, but recognition of the reality that the West Bank and Gaza are two separate entities led by forces currently unable to breach the differences between them in any meaningful way. One is for a tactical, cynical, temporary cease-fire, the other for serious peace negotiations and an equitable settlement. One is Islamic fundamentalist, the other more secular and traditional. The contrast could not be starker. Four attempts at conciliation between the sides brokered by the Saudis and others in the Arab world all failed. The fifth came in April 2011, when the Egyptians claimed agreement on conciliation between Hamas and Fatah had been reached. In reality the "agreement" was the result of secret talks between the new Egyptian regime—which now included the Muslim Brotherhood—and Hamas. The PA on the West Bank was not consulted, did not take part in the wording of the agreement, and was taken by surprise when it was announced. Though furious, skeptical, and at risk of its relations with Israel and the United States, the PA, however, had to go along with the announcement on supposed reconciliation. Who, after all, could be against national unity while at the same time asking the world to recognize a Palestinian State? But in reality the chances of genuine conciliation were as distant, if not more so, than ever. This agreement, like those before it, will likely be stillborn.

A settlement with the Palestinians over the West Bank is not going to be easy. Neither side will ever be fully happy, recent history having created modern Israel where Palestine should be, and Palestine where Israel should be. Ashkelon, Jaffa, Haifa, and Acre on the Mediterranean are all associated with the Palestinians, while the heart of biblical Israel is Judea and Samaria, Hebron, Shiloh.

Still, the idea of two states is supported by the Americans, the Europeans, almost the entire Arab world, and, critically, by right-wing Israeli Prime Minister Binyamin Netanyahu, now in his second term, as well as the country's main opposition party, Kadima. Yet in the absence of serious negotiations with Israel, the Palestinian leadership was planning to embark on a new path: to seek international recognition of a Palestinian state in the West Bank, Gaza, and East Jerusalem at the United Nations in September 2011. Speaking to an audience at the Institute for National Security Studies at Tel Aviv University in January 2011, Defense Minister Ehud Barak said that by the end of 2011 Israel could expect "a tsunami of international support for a Palestinian state," and that the country had best prepare itself for the reality of the situation.

No one denies that the path to an agreement is complicated and that unraveling a ball of thorns can prick one's fingers, but the problem is not beyond resolution. Few international problems have such well-defined solutions. Israel will be at war with Iran and its proxies long after an agreement is reached with the Palestinians. What is required to make it happen is leadership, a cool hand on the wheel of state navigating through rough waters. We all know there is land on the horizon.

According to senior Palestinians and Israelis, if the sides were to sit down with a mandate from their respective electorates, an agreement could be reached in months. Much paperwork has been done since Oslo, through years of interaction at almost every level of government. Dozens of committees were set up after Oslo, dealing with issues from insurance protocols to currency and taxes, security arrangements and border access. There is little more to do than open the closet, dust off the files, and apply the knowledge. The Clinton Parameters set out guidelines for even the most complicated and sensitive of subjects, including Jerusalem and the refugees, with clarity and reason. Over the years I have attended dozens of conflict resolution conferences, or second-track meetings, as they are called, with Palestinians, Syrians, and even Iranians, having almost common cause with the Palestinians even in the worst of times, such as the Second Intifada. The Syrians were always cool and the Iranians would avoid one-on-one contact, fearful of retribution back home. In Istanbul in 2000, the editor of the English-language *Iran Times* disappeared into an Iranian jail on "charges" of immorality, after having dinner with a group of journalists including a few of us from Israel, and a professor at one of the major universities stopped e-mail contact recently, after a message saying it was better that way. With the Palestinians, no matter how much we shouted at one another, there was a level of rationality to the debate: There were always points of agreement, and always shared lunches and dinners at which things were hammered out in calmer, if no less intense, tones. We all knew the realities, the clay with which we had to work, and we all shared the same fear: the longer peace is delayed the farther away are the chances for a two-state solution. Demography is moving Israel to the right and the Palestinians to fundamentalism and exodus. Time is on neither side.

* * *

In the summer of 2005 I went to see Tzipi Livni, then the minister of absorption in Ariel Sharon's government. It was just before the Gaza disengagement and she had just arrived from a cabinet meeting where the dimensions of the Israeli withdrawal from Gaza were discussed, the issue being whether to retain troops on the Gaza-Egypt border to prevent smuggling, as the military was demanding, or to order a total withdrawal, as Sharon preferred. She opted for a clean cut. With the military, she explained, they always needed a little bit more to do their job: "Before we know it we will be back in Gaza, up to our ears."

The complete withdrawal from Gaza, agreeing to uproot and destroy settlements, to throw Jews out of their homes, was not an easy decision for Livni. It went counter to every political bone in her body. Her background was deeply Revisionist, the extreme right of the Israeli political sphere. Her father, Eitan, had been a member of the Knesset from the Herut party that had as its credo a Jewish state on both sides of the River Jordan. I told her that I remembered him well, from when I was a Knesset reporter, as tall, strong, and unsmiling with red hair and a fiery temperament.

She confirmed the memory, walked to the bookshelf, and took down a slim volume, a biography of her father. On the inside page was a black and white picture of her father's gravestone. Deeply etched in the granite, above his name, birth date, and date of death, was the symbol and slogan of Lehi, the pre-1948 underground: a clenched hand firmly holding a rifle over a map of Israel that included the West Bank and all of trans-Jordan. That was what he wanted on his tombstone, she said, adding, "to think, his daughter is now prepared to compromise and uproot settlements. I can almost hear his shout from the grave."

Tzipi Livni was not alone in her metamorphosis from the ideological right to the center, subscribing to Ariel Sharon's view that the only way for Israel to survive as a Jewish and democratic state was to shed the territories. Ehud Olmert, also of old Likud stock, who succeeded Sharon as prime minister after Sharon's stroke, entered into negotiations with the Palestinians, offering, according to him, 93 percent of the West Bank and all of Gaza, an equitable land swap to make up the difference, and international oversight of the holy sites of Jerusalem. Olmert openly declared that Israel needed to end its role as occupier. Though a former mayor of Jerusalem who spoke incessantly about a united Jerusalem forever, he changed his tune as prime minister, offering the Palestinians control over all the villages to the east that until then had been considered integral parts of a united Jerusalem, and proposing an international trusteeship for the Old City and Holy Basin. The list of new pragmatists who moved from the Likud to the center, from "not one inch" to a two-state solution, is long and respectable, dotted with the "princes," as they were called, the children of old established Likud families who went into politics believing staunchly in the Land of Israel. These were generally well-schooled, well-mannered, and successful people, many of them lawyers, who, as they assumed positions of responsibility in government as their careers advanced, understood that Israel needed to consolidate to effectively deal with the challenges it faced. A scion of this "breed" is Dan Meridor, who has served in several Likud-led governments as minister of justice, finance, and as cabinet secretary to Menachem Begin. He was molded for politics by his father, Yaakov, a lawyer, former member of the Knesset, close associate of Begin, and stalwart member of the Lehi underground and the right-wing nationalist Herut party.

In November 2010, now a minister of atomic affairs and intelligence and deputy prime minister in Netanyahu's second government, a key and sensitive post, Meridor admitted to a dinner audience at the Begin Heritage Center in Jerusalem, of all places, that he himself had come full circle from believing in a Land of Israel from the sea to the Jordan River, to understanding that only a two-state solution could save Israel. He explained how, as a democrat, he and others on the Right thought the Palestinians would be happy to be Israeli citizens and the Jews would always be a majority. But demographic realities and the Second Intifada left an indelible mark on his thinking. He came to realize that it is impossible to have it all. The choice is blatantly clear: between Greater Israel or Democratic and Jewish Israel.

As with the peace treaty with Egypt in 1979, when Menachem Begin gave back Sinai to the Egyptians, so a new generation of ideological rightists had moved to the center, wanting to end a status quo they judged as untenable.

At the end of 2010 the majority of the Knesset would have supported peace moves with the West Bank. Coalitions come and go in Israeli politics, but no matter how one moved the chairs around in the second Netanyahu government, there was a majority for dialogue and, failing that, more unilateralism.

Along the seam dividing Israel and the West Bank, more or less following the 1967 boundary except for some notable deviations, is a security barrier built by Israel. By the end of 2010 about 60 percent of it was completed, running mostly on the Palestinian side of the 1967 boundary and, in some cases, protruding deep into Palestinian territory. The barrier, constructed of fences, walls, trenches, and early-warning systems, and policed by cameras and patrols, will eventually be seven hundred kilometers long and will have cost the country hundreds of millions of dollars.

It is ugly, like a scar through the land, but it has brought down suicide bombing to virtually zero, though continued military and intelligence operations, the isolation of Gaza, changed Hamas tactics, and responsible government on the West Bank have contributed to this as well. It was built by Sharon at the height of the suicide bombings, very much against the prime minister's will, as it implied a permanent statement about where Israel considered its future border to be. It also created a furor among the Israeli settlers left on the "other" side.

In building the barrier, Sharon gave in to his internal security chief at the time, Avi Dichter, who said the barrier was an essential national security project, and to the public's demand for greater personal security, something that was fast becoming an electoral issue. It was also an expression of frustration that Israel would never be able to come to a negotiated solution with the Palestinians—a monument, almost, to the failure of peace.

The Wall, as those who oppose the barrier call it, even though 90 percent of it is a fence, is hated by the Palestinians, and with good cause. It runs through their lands, cutting off families from their fields, children from their schools, Palestinians from working in Israel, and hundreds of thousands of Palestinians on the Israeli side of the barrier, including in East Jerusalem, from the other side.

The security threat to settlers living beyond the barrier led to multiple Israeli roadblocks on the West Bank, and has severely hampered West Bank trade from Israel and the sea. The barrier creates almost as much a stranglehold on the West Bank as there is on Gaza, though the Jordanian border is open to Palestinians, unlike Gaza's border with Egypt for much of the past few years, though Egypt has allowed limited travel since May 2011.

But more than anything the barrier—and the Palestinians understand this—is a dam of last resort against the demographic threat, a statement by Israel that if we cannot find a formula for peace, we will have to live with a wall between us.

Eitan Livni's dream of an Israel in all the land promised to Jacob up to the Euphrates River has long passed. So, for many, has the idea of Israel retaining all of the West Bank in enmity with the Palestinians forever. If it hands over the West Bank, Israel is down to its last line; there is no more territory to concede or concessions to be made. If there is no peace, Israelis again will be living behind a wall, a self-imposed ghetto, and the Palestinians in a never-never land between occupation and independence, in the shadow of a physical barrier that may not be impregnable to missiles and mortars but, as a last resort, will certainly help ensure the Jewish nature of the state for generations to come.

NINE

The Threat
from the North

The North of Israel is breathtakingly beautiful all year round, but in the spring it is magnificent. Blossoms carpet the landscape and the fields are green and lush, grapes heavy on the vine. Over half a billion birds migrate through the Galilee each year and the Hula, once a swamp, is now a national park thriving with wildlife, both flora and fauna. Its draining at the turn of the twentieth century was seen as a pioneering Zionist achievement; now it is known to have been a massive ecological mistake to remove the natural filter that used to ensure the purity of the water flowing through the swamps to the Kinneret, Israel's main water supply.

The beauty of the area, however, belies security realities there with the Galilee wedged between Syria and Lebanon.

Israel conquered the Golan from the Syrians in 1967, and again in 1973. A year later there was a UN-brokered cease-fire between the sides and despite the enmity between them, the border has remained quiet since then. Syria under the Assads, on the other hand, has been at the center of the Middle East's axis of evil and, despite attempts at supposed peacemaking with Israel, demonstrably remains so. It is a conduit to antigovernment forces in Iraq, a base for rejectionist and fundamentalist Islamic nationalists, including Hamas and the Islamic Jihad, and both a supplier and conduit of weapons, training, money, and support to Hezbollah.

Successive Israeli governments have been in a dilemma about making peace with Syria. Now it is probably too late.

On the face of things, it ought to be far easier for Israel to give back the Golan in return for peace with Syria, than the West Bank to the Palestinians. There are only twenty settlements up there, including one town, Katzrin, with a population of 7,000, almost half the total number of settlers on the Heights. Almost all the settlers on the Golan would accept proper and decent compensation if they had to move. There is an anti-give-back-the-Golan movement in Israel, but it arouses none of the passion of the West Bank and would not be a serious impediment to implementing a peace treaty. The 20,000 Druze who live on the Golan, 90 percent of whom have refused Israeli citizenship, would be more than happy (they say) to return to Syria and be united with the 80,000 Druze who live on the Syrian side of the border with whom they have had to communicate by shouting from hilltops for over forty years.

Israel has serious intelligence assets on the Golan as well as valuable training grounds for its armored, artillery, and infantry forces that can maneuver freely given the scarcity of population there. It is the source of 12 percent of Israel's water, and strategically overlooks the Galilee, but these issues can be overcome. Israel can increase its production of desalinated water from the Mediterranean, and the conservation of water, major strides having been made in both, and a peace treaty between Israel and Syria would require Syrian forces to be withdrawn deep inside the country, far enough from Israel's border to not pose a threat.

Intelligence posts on the Hermon, the highest spot in Israeli-controlled territory, are Israel's eyes and ears on Hezbollah and guard the avenues of attack from Iran and Syria, and all over the Golan. On hills like Bental and others, antennae sprout like bamboo, picking up signals and whatever else intelligence posts do. The experts, however, say that in today's world these assets are not as vital as they used to be; static satellites, drones, and other means can now carry out these tasks, and to better effect. Two former chiefs of staff, Yitzhak Rabin and Ehud Barak, have been prepared to give up the Golan for real peace. "The depth of our withdrawal will be equal to the depth of peace," Rabin told me in an interview on November 2, 1995, just days before he was assassinated. At Shepherdstown in January 2000, Barak came within an inch of signing an agreement with the Syrians that would have seen the Golan return to Syria, intelligence posts included.

Peace has ostensibly always broken down over the issue of whether the Syrians would have a foothold on the Kinneret— the Sea of Galilee. Hafez al-Assad demanded it, claiming he wanted to have a barbecue on its shores with his feet in the water, and the Israelis have always been reluctant to have Syria anywhere near the country's major water resource. In truth neither of the sides found making peace a major imperative; they could live without it. For Syria the Golan was an issue of pride, the area always having been left to the Druze, who would remain there anyway, and for Israel the complications of making peace often seemed to outweigh the benefits of remaining on the Golan. Had Rabin not been assassinated, perhaps he and the "old fox," Assad, would have come to an agreement. Warren Christopher, secretary of state in the first Clinton administration, made countless trips between the sides and held, according to one American participant, "bladder-breaking" sessions with Assad, and came close to success before Amir's bullet changed the course of history. By the time Barak considered signing the Shepherdstown accords in January 2000, Assad was six months from death, and more concerned about succession than peace with Israel. If one wants to be generous with Barak, one could argue that this was the main reason for his balking at the last minute. He knew he would have Assad's signature on the document, but he also knew Assad would not be around to implement it. It was not unreasonable to think that Assad's death could have sparked a period of instability that would have made the agreement worthless. Above all, Barak's domestic situation was precarious with his coalition collapsing, making it unlikely he could muster up the support to back an agreement with the Syrians.

The inability of the sides to make peace has not meant that the situation has remained static. When still firmly in power, Syrian president Bashar Assad made overtures toward peace, first through the Americans and later with the Turks, and still dangles the hope from time to time, but in the background he has been preparing for war. In the nonconventional realm, Syria has continued to invest heavily in chemical weapons, or a "poor man's nuclear bomb," as Israeli analysts have called Syria's chemical-capable missile force. The real shock, however, came at midnight September 6, 2007, when the world discovered that Syria was on its way to acquiring a rich man's bomb as well. Initially mystery surrounded the destruction of an unnamed Syrian facility somewhere in the mountains of the Deir Ez-Zor province. Within days, however, it was clear that Israeli jets with American and Turkish connivance, the latter allowing Israeli jets to fly through Turkish airspace on their way to Syria, had destroyed a nascent Syrian plutonium enrichment plant secretly acquired from North Korea. The focus of Assad's force-building, however, has been missile acquisition, anti-aircraft missiles to blunt the force of the Israeli air force, and offensive long- and medium-range missiles to leapfrog the Golan Heights and Israel's ground forces and cause major damage to Israel's heartland. With these Assad has invested heavily in early-warning systems and replaced most of his liquid-fuel missiles with solid-fuel ones. Because liquid missile fuels are corrosive, they must be fueled just before use, a process that can take a few days. Solid-fuel missiles are always ready to go. Assad has invested almost nothing in his ground forces, understanding that they are of minimal use in the current theater, and the air force has steadily declined as the aircraft Syria wanted from Russia, the MiG-31, were denied and those already deployed gradually became obsolete and poorly maintained.

Overall, Israeli strategists believe they can deal with the Syrian threat but are not complacent about it. Syria's ability to absorb new technologies has been limited, and as war becomes more sophisticated, Israel's advantage over the Syrians increases. In 1973 the Israeli air force was plagued by Syrian Soviet-supplied anti-aircraft missiles. By 1982, in the opening stages of the

Israel-Lebanon war, the Israeli air force destroyed seventeen of the nineteen Syrian SAM-6 missile batteries deployed in the Beka'a Valley. They also downed twenty-nine Syrian aircraft in one day, with no Israeli losses. By the end of the war, eighty-six Syrian aircraft had been downed, with no Israeli losses. This was achieved despite the substantial investment the Syrians had made in technology between 1973 and 1982; Israel had found the Achilles' heel of the Syrian air force. Israeli aircraft were equipped with over-the-horizon radar, which had limited capacity because of their small size but allowed pilots to see much farther than the naked eye. Syrian pilots, on the other hand, were vectored into eye contact with the enemy by controllers using powerful ground-based radar, which could see much farther than those in Israeli cockpits but were useless if controllers could not communicate with the fighters they were supposed to guide into action. By jamming contact between controllers on the ground and pilots in the air, Israel made the Syrians sitting ducks. In the twenty-five years since then, despite Assad's penchant for the Internet, by any yardstick one can assume that the technological gap between the two countries has widened. Syria, dependent on Soviet-type weapon systems, has regressed. Russian military technologies have slipped behind those of the West, and while Russia denies the Syrians some advanced weapons, Israel and America work closely together, including America's agreement in 2010 to supply Israel with super-advanced F-35 stealth fighters and new-realm technologies that come with the aircraft.

Israeli planners continue to take seriously the idea of a Syrian threat, especially one launched in tandem with attacks from Lebanon and Gaza. The discovery of the plutonium reactor was yet another indicator that Syria was not sitting on its hands. To-gether with Hezbollah and Hamas, and, even without them, the Syrians can hurt Israel badly, especially if they have the element of surprise. To do so, however, would be suicidal. Israel has made it clear to Assad that among the hundreds of targets that have been programmed into Israeli attack systems, his family and all they possess will be prime among them; Alawite rule, the minority sect that now rules Syria, will be removed from Syria for generations to come. On the other hand, Israel is fairly well prepared to absorb a conventional attack. Many homes have sealed and protected rooms built by law, and there are ample neighborhood bomb shel-ters for those who don't. Major damage could be caused by a salvo of several hundred missiles fired in a short period of time, but Israel would not take long to hit back, so a Syrian attack can be assumed to be limited in time and scope, little being achieved after the first missiles have landed. Israel's response would be mas-sive and sustained. A chemical attack by Syria would warrant a nonconventional Israeli response, something the Syrians would not even want to begin to consider, one supposes.

Therefore, in conventional terms, while Syria remains a factor in any strategic equation, the real incentive, if any, for Israel to make peace with Syria would be to draw Syria away from the sphere of Iran, Hezbollah, the Islamic Jihad, and Hamas, and to stop being a negative player in Iraq. The military benefits to Israel of peace with Syria are ambivalent, but changing the regional strategic bal-ance by drawing Syria away from the rejectionists and fundamen-talists and into the moderate camp would be a major achievement.

When Assad first came into power, there was some hope that he would take Syria down a new path. He began his term by releasing political prisoners, allowing some freedom of political expression, and loosening up on Internet use. But the "old guard" soon put him back on track and away from any radical ideas that could jeopardize their hold on power. They also steered him in the direction of his father's old tricks, pulling the strings in Lebanon, helping antigovernment forces in Iraq, and acting as Iran's messenger boy in the region, delivering arms and ammunition to Hezbollah and others. Hezbollah also underestimated Israel's response to the war it started in 2006. Its head, Hassan Nasrallah, said as much in an open interview after the war, stating that had he known the ferocity of Israel's reaction, he would have handled the situation differently. The war was sparked by a Hezbollah raid over the Israeli border and the killing and kidnapping of soldiers. It ended with Hezbollah's strongholds in Beirut, its missile arsenals, its underground infrastructure in the South, and much of its command structure in ruins. Along with the punishment heaped upon Hezbollah, Lebanon's infrastructure was bombed and destroyed, including refineries, roads, and bridges. By 2010 Hezbollah, with Iranian and Syrian help, had bounced back again. The organization now has some 45,000 missiles stockpiled, some with a range of two hundred kilometers or more, and much of its military infrastructure is re-embedded in 250 Shiite villages in southern Lebanon, within kilometers of the Israeli border. In reality, though, the organization has been seriously weakened. Nasrallah has yet to come out from his underground shelter, and he speaks to his minions via videotape. With Israel withdrawn to a UN-recognized boundary, other than one problematic tiny enclave called Ghajar—Sheba Farms—Hezbollah has lost its primary reason for conflict. Now that it has taken on a high-profile political role in Lebanese politics, the only political party in any so-called democracy in the world with a private army, it has to tread carefully.

Israel has also had time to focus on Hezbollah, which is now defined by the military as Israel's number-one regional enemy but until 2006 was considered a tactical problem, not a strategic one. In 2006, at the outbreak of the war, Israeli military planners had 189 Hezbollah targets in their sights. Israeli military sources now claim to have 4,000 to 6,000, and to prove their point, in March 2011 the Israeli military provided the *Washington Post* with a map detailing 950 Hezbollah sites in southern Lebanon the Israelis considered "hostile." Hezbollah had thought these secret, and knowing they had been revealed could not have been a source of much joy to either Hezbollah or their Iranian patrons.

Hezbollah embarrassed the Israeli army in the 2006 war. The taking out of a highly sophisticated missile boat on the second day of the war and the heavy Israeli casualties in southern Lebanon, together with the war's crippling effect on Israel's interior with cities and towns being paralyzed by Hezbollah fire, did much to tarnish the IDF's image with the public. A new chief of staff was appointed, commissions of inquiry held, and conclusions drawn, and a humbled and angry military command sat down and planned how to best exact their revenge. If one is to believe them, they are just waiting for an excuse to level the playing field, which in their mind means pretty much leveling Lebanon's national infrastructure and as many of Hezbollah's assets as can be identified.

The military has redefined the way it sees Lebanon. It has gone from being seen as a "victim" country and unwilling battlefield for Israel's wars with others to being a country governed by a troika of enemies: Hezbollah, Syria, and Iran. The Shiites, Hezbollah's constituency, are the country's largest ethnic group, at 30 percent of the population, and unlike the Christians and Sunnis, are united and loyal to Hezbollah. They control Parliament, have an army more sophisticated, better trained, and better financed than the Lebanese army, and through loyalists control much of the Lebanese military forces as well. Unbelievably, despite this, until March 2011 the Lebanese army continued to receive over $100 million in U.S. aid annually, which is not unlike America's provision of Stinger missiles to the Taliban in the late 1970s.

The Israeli command is not threatened by either Hezbollah or Syria. They feel they have responses to both. In both cases the strategy is one of disproportionate response to any attack. They feel they have enough early warning, even with the technical advances both Hezbollah and Syria have made. They have contingency plans that cover all of Israel's airfields being attacked simultaneously and have developed an array of attack weapons that do not depend on the air force, mainly drone-based and highly accurate and destructive cruise missiles that can be launched from land and sea. Most of the Israeli air force is protected by bunkers and would survive any initial attack. Runways are quickly repaired, and for emergencies the country has built some major highways specifically as alternate runways should the country's airfields be attacked. If attacked, Israel will launch a massive counterstrike with cruise missiles and drones on hundreds of predetermined targets with pinpoint accuracy.

Israel's strategic response to the two arms embracing the Galilee and from which it is threatened comprises heavy investment in protecting the home front, and a massive, disproportionate, and crippling response to any attack. And everybody knows it. Israel has spared no expense in allowing the military to develop the necessary technology and strategies to defend the country. This investment goes from outer space to specially trained tactical teams on the ground. As with Iran, when Israel's mind is focused on what is perceived as a strategic threat, as Hezbollah has become, it finds the answers it needs. Hezbollah would do well to look at the deployment of the Israeli Iron Dome anti-rocket system in southern Israel with its 90 percent kill ratio, as demonstrated in southern Israel in April 2011, and the offensive means Israel intends to unleash if provoked. The war of 2006 was a seminal moment in Israel's relationship with Hezbollah, and given that five years later its leader, Sheikh Sayyed Hassan Nasrallah, has not emerged from his underground bunker, he may have understood the implications of this change better than most.

The internal turmoil that hit Syria, as with the other dictatorships in the Middle East in early 2011, has weakened the regime considerably, if not heralded its end—though probably only after a long, bitter, and bloody internal conflict. Assad has used his security forces brutally against the demonstrators, firing directly into crowds, arresting hundreds, executing soldiers who refused to obey orders, breaking kneecaps of young demonstrators with hammers and rifle butts. By May 2011, almost a thousand people had been killed amid escalating violence that only looked as if it could get worse. Even before the current wave of internal unrest, it was the assessment in Israel that despite his involvement with every negative force in the Middle East and beyond, Bashar Assad does not want war. While some Arab leaders respond to internal crisis by goading Israel into a war, as has been the case with Hamas in Gaza and Hezbollah on the Lebanese border, Syria would have little to gain from it. Syria is in America's sights because of its negative role in Iraq and involvement with Jihadist forces, and it is doubtful whether Iran would come to its aid. If it did so, it would risk giving Israel a legitimate excuse to attack Iran's nuclear facilities, and the 45,000 missiles it has stockpiled with Hezbollah in Lebanon. And now, with its internal problems, a war with Israel is surely the last thing on Assad's mind.

As a country, Lebanon has absolutely no reason to go to war. It is finally seeing some economic growth, 7 percent in 2010, and a revival in tourism with over two million people, mainly from Arab states, visiting in 2010. Much of the damage from 2006 has been repaired and neither the Sunnis nor the Christians, who make up over 50 percent of the country's population, want to see it go down again. Hezbollah understands Israel's message of disproportionate response and, after seeing what Israel did in Gaza in the winter of 2008–2009, understands that it will not be saved by hiding in civilian infrastructure. Israel's plan is to give villagers in the South fair warning to leave their homes, and then destroy the command posts, trenches, ammunition dumps, and logistical supplies hidden under them. That will be the price of war, and the Shiites, Hezbollah's core supporters, who live in the south of Lebanon, will pay the price, as they have before. There is not a single Israeli on Lebanese soil. Hezbollah has no reason to attack. If it does, it will have to explain the consequences to the relatives of the dead, the displaced, and those surveying the rubble caused by the organization's folly.

* * *

Israel's Northern Command is nestled in the hills just north of the mystical city of Safed in the Galilee. It stands on a peak above the pastoral village of Birya, with a stunning view of the Galilee and the Golan, a steep cliff to the east and Israel's largest forest to the west. The command compound is militarily neat with a sense of order prevailing, whitewash evident everywhere, from stones marking paths to the stumps of trees. The command offices are wood and stone barrackslike huts, presumably left over from the British, though upgraded with air-conditioning and other amenities. To the north one can see an electronic listening post, hardly camouflaged at all, and to the east the entrance to "Israel's Noah's Ark," the underground command post impervious to any attack, including a nonconventional one, where the real work is done. If Israel is attacked with nuclear weapons, it is from here the next generation of Israelis will emerge.

The O.C. Northern Command is the only general in the Israeli defense forces who can go to war without permission from a higher authority. He cannot strike preemptively without a cabinet decision, but when faced with an immediate threat he can respond immediately with the means at his disposal, which one assumes includes cruise missiles and attack drones.

At the end of 2010 Gadi Eizenkot was the head of Northern Command. He had taken over in 2006 from Udi Adam, himself the son of a general, whose performance in the Lebanese war was found to be lacking. Eizenkot is a tree trunk of a man with a thick neck and broad, squat shoulders. He is known as a no-nonsense general with broad experience. He commanded the Golani infantry brigade and Israeli forces on the West Bank and served as head of military operations. He had also done a stint as military secretary to the prime minister, making him familiar with the inner workings of government. One November afternoon, after first touring the base and walking through an avenue dedicated to former commanders of the North, each represented by a huge rock with their names inscribed, Eizenkot found time to give a briefing. Standing squarely and rocklike himself between two huge LCD screens, he spelled out his doctrine of disproportionate response and predicted that any future war would be decided in four or five days, even though dealing with the source problem could take longer, depending on what Israel decided to do. I had listened to similar briefings in the same room before the 1973 war and again in 1982, when an equally adamantine Ariel Sharon outlined his "limited" excursion into Lebanon, so I had good reason to be skeptical. In 1973 the boasts were proved hollow by the surprise of the Yom Kippur attack, and in 1982 Sharon blatantly lied about his intentions. But this time, somehow, Eizenkot's message rang true. It made sense. Though logic and intelligence reports indicate that neither Syria nor Hezbollah have an interest in another war now, miscalculation is always possible, especially when you are not master of your own destiny and are in the hands of Syria and Iran. Eizenkot says Israel is prepared, and I for one believe him.

On the wall of the briefing room, framed and written on parchment, not unlike the Ten Commandments, were the ten rules of engagement Israeli officers were to remember when planning their operations: stick by your mission; maintain morale; take the initiative; use cunning and deception; concentrate your attack; guard yourself; use force to its maximum; ensure mobility and continuity; have depth and reserve; and be simple to operate.

They all seemed to conform to the strategies being outlined by Eizenkot now, and those used by King David 3,000 years ago when he killed Goliath. David came focused on his mission, made his people believe that he could slaughter the giant, selected three pebbles from a stream, sought the weak spot in the giant's armor, and concentrated all his efforts there. He had a plan, kept it simple, and used surprise and well-trained accuracy to do the job. Having killed a leopard attacking his sheep, he knew he could fell the giant. By the end of 2010, Hezbollah no longer seemed quite the threat it had been before. Syria, though allied with Iran and increasingly with Turkey, remains weak and indecisive, unsure of its destination while its Alawite leadership seeks mainly to retain power.

One has the sense that the status quo to Israel's north will continue for a while. Or there could be war. In either case, Israel's survival will be tested but not threatened. The country may be badly mauled, but it will survive and its neighbors will pay a price they will long remember. Part of the Eizenkot doctrine is that if deterrence fails and a war breaks out, the goal would be not only to win the war but to damage the enemy to such an extent that it would take years before they could even think of going to war again.

When Eizenkot said it, he almost looked as though he wished the enemy would initiate a war.

TEN

Israel's New War:
Legitimacy

Ever since its creation, Israel has had to fight to be seen as legitimate, in itself strange considering that the country was voted into being by the United Nations as part of a post–Second World War redistribution of territories under the British mandate. It has one of the most legitimate origins of any nation-state.

After the War of Independence, the country was generally loved as an underdog, romanticized in books like Leon Uris's *Exodus*, which had, I believe, a greater Zionist impact on my generation of Jews than the Bible, Herzl, and A. D. Gordon collectively. Lingering guilt over the Holocaust made it politically incorrect to attack Israel in polite circles, outside the Arab world and the former Soviet Union, where some felt that Hitler had not done a good enough job.

After the Six-Day War, things became euphoric. Many saw Israel's victory as the Scriptures coming to life before their eyes,

Ezekiel's prophecies realized; others took pride in how a small nation had stood up to its foes and with stealth and courage, slaughtered the new Philistines and their mocking giant, Egypt's Gamal Abdel Nasser. There was a slump in popularity when Arabs unleashed the oil weapon in the 1970s, causing prices to rise and with them anti-Israel sentiment the world over.

Israel's shares went up a bit with the rescue of the passengers of an Air France airliner with 248 people aboard, hijacked by Palestinian terrorists on June 27, 1976. A week later, on July 4, Israeli commandoes landed at Entebbe airport, over 4,000 kilometers away, and spirited the hostages safely away, with only one Israeli soldier being killed, Yoni Netanyahu, Binyamin Netanyahu's younger brother, the commander of the operation. The 1978 peace accords with Egypt made Israel more palatable to the moderate Arab world and pushed up the country's popularity again after a few problematic years the world had with Israel's first right-wing government, headed by Menachem Begin, and, specifically, with his settlement policies on the West Bank.

Since then, however, it has been mostly downhill. Israel's various campaigns in Lebanon, starting with the Litani operation in 1978 that gave Israel an additional conquest, southern Lebanon, followed by the First Lebanese War in 1982, and the Sabra and Shatila massacres by Israel's Christian Phalange allies, inestimably damaged how Israel was perceived in the world. While not directly involved in the massacre, Israel turned a blind eye to the slaughter of hundreds, some say thousands, of innocent Palestinians by the Phalange over a weekend.

But it was the intifada from 1987 to 1993 that brought to the world the reality of Israel's occupation of the territories, brutally caught for posterity in film by a CBS television crew that had Israeli soldiers breaking the arms of young Palestinians they suspected of throwing rocks. Continuous pictures of Israeli tanks and soldiers armed to the hilt acting against Palestinian civilians with brute force, the arrogance of the armed settlers who seemed impervious to any law, free to do their own will in the occupied territories, and the emergence of articulate Palestinian spokespeople, such as Sari Nusseibeh, Faisal Husseini, and Hanan Ashrawi, all took their toll on Israel's image.

When the Second Intifada broke out in September 2000, the French news channel, France 2, broadcast a fifty-nine-second clip on its evening news that literally lost Israel the war in the eyes of the international community almost before it had begun. Muhammad Dura, a twelve-year-old, and his father, Jamal, were pictured huddling behind a concrete cylinder, caught in the crossfire between Israeli and Palestinian Authority forces at the Netzarim junction in Gaza. The twelve-year-old was clinging to his father's back, while his father waved wildly to attract help. Then came a volley of fire and, on camera, Muhammad Dura was killed. The footage was shot by Talal Abu Rahma, a Palestinian freelancer, and from the footage alone it was far from clear whose bullets had killed the boy—Israel's or those of the Palestinians. But without being at the scene of the incident itself, Charles Enderlin, the veteran France 2 reporter based in Jerusalem, broadcast that Dura had been "a target of fire from Israeli positions," a charge never proved and often disputed, but nevertheless one that reverberated around the world, causing Dura to be declared a martyr in the Arab world, a symbol of Israeli brutality and force against an occupied people. Though the Palestinians used suicide bombers with devastating results, through the years of bitter warfare, Israel was seen as the aggressor, and there was little empathy or sympathy with either its cause or its predicament. The occupation and its implementation was seen as the evil, not the suicide bombings and shooting attacks that claimed the lives of some 1,100 Israeli civilians and left thousands more maimed and crippled for life.

So indelible was the Dura footage that at a conference at Tel Aviv University in early 2002, former prime ministers Ehud Barak and Binyamin Netanyahu, in uncoordinated lectures on Israel's public diplomacy in the Second Intifada, given five hours apart, both mentioned how Dura had featured in their talks with world leaders. Both Barak and Netanyahu related how some European prime ministers and presidents had the photograph of Dura huddling behind his father on their desks, and no sooner had they sat down and regardless of any prepared agenda, the first thing discussed were charges of Israel's use of excessive force against the Palestinians.

During the Second Intifada there was a realization in Israel that public diplomacy had become a strategic issue. Beyond the Dura affair, in 2001 in Durban, South Africa, the UN sponsored the World Conference against Racism, Racial Discrimination, Xenophobia, and Related Intolerance. It was chaired by former Irish president Mary Robinson, the UN high commissioner on human rights at the time of the conference. The intention was to deal with slavery, a major topic on the African agenda, and the situation in Sudan, Darfur, Rwanda, and other disaster areas.

But after quick lip service to the slavery issue, the entire conference then focused on one subject: Israel. Israel the apartheid state, Israel the racist state, Israel the noxious state, even Israel the Nazi state, with the blue Star of David twisted into a swastika on the background of the Israeli flag. This was not happening outside in a demonstration of skinheads and Jihadists, but in the plenum, with the world's diplomats in attendance and Robinson in the chair. In the end, Darfur, Sudan, and Rwanda were all ignored, while Israel was declared "racist," leading the United States to walk out and the delegates to decide to meet again in the future and assess how sanctions against Israel were doing. The vote was passed by a sizable majority with the delegates from Burkina Faso, St. Vincent and the Grenadines, Trinidad and Tobago, Tuvalu, and Barbados all convinced that they were doing the right thing.

On the eve of the conference, a terrorist had exploded himself in downtown Jerusalem, killing 15 people and injuring 130 more. His five-kilogram bomb, packed with nails, bolts, and nuts, left many injured for life. Not a word was said in Durban in condemnation, nor did the incident stop thousands of South African Muslims from marching through the streets of the city shouting "death to the Jews, death to the Jews," while the delegates pondered Israeli racism inside.

The Durban conference was soon lost in the dust of 9/11, which happened three days later, leaving the world a lot less sanguine about suicide bombers, but it struck a chord in the Israeli policy community.

Less than six months later, Israel's image would suffer yet another bashing, although again the incident in question was a direct result of a suicide bombing that should have brought Israel support and sympathy. Instead it became a launching pad for another vociferous campaign against the country. In response to the deadly Netanya Passover suicide attack in 2002, Israeli forces reentered the West Bank. One of the hardest nuts for the Israelis to crack were Palestinian resistance units in Jenin, from where a large number of suicide bombers had been dispatched over the years. The refugee camp there was densely populated, booby traps were expected, and it was easy for the terrorists to move in and out of the narrow alleys where Israeli armored vehicles could not maneuver. Israel was concerned by the potential loss of life to its own forces, but military planners were also acutely aware of the "Muhammad Dura factor," to the point that then defense minister Binyamin Ben-Eliezer refused an army request to use F-16s to bomb targets at the entrance of the refugee camp, for fear of being accused of using "disproportionate force" and provoking another barrage of damaging international criticism. That decision cost Israel thirteen dead soldiers, but that fact went unknown and unnoticed as messages started to leave the Jenin camp via cell phones, some of them with video clips, claiming that Israel had committed a massacre in the camps.

Soon the world media, led by Al Jazeera with CNN and the others not far behind, started reporting rumors of the massacres with figures of people killed running into the hundreds and sometimes thousands. Israel had barred media from covering the battle, supposedly because it wanted to hide from the world what it was doing, and what filled the airwaves instead of reporting from responsible correspondents were rumors and manipulated evidence that propagated the lie of a massacre that never happened. In seventeen days of violent urban fighting, fifty-two Palestinians were killed, twenty-six of them armed fighters. Israel suffered a total of twenty-three dead, despite using better equipment. During the fighting, Israel and the Red Cross had talks that allowed for freedom of movement for ambulances, while Israel provided a generator to the Jenin hospital and blankets for those caught in the battle, hardly a massacre.

Israel had no one but itself to blame for the media fallout over Jenin. Trade unions in Scandinavia refused to offload Israeli ships, and condemnation of Israel was rife on every corner, including from liberal members of the Jewish community who thought that Israel was going too far in trying to smother the intifada. In the Arab world Al Jazeera's sensationalistic reporting had a major effect on the vilification of Israel, making it particularly difficult for the Egyptians and Jordanians to remain neutral. No matter how much proof Israel produced that no massacre had happened, the damage was done.

There were other instances during the Second Intifada where Israel did itself enormous harm because of its inability to explain its case effectively. Sheikh Ahmed Yassin, the founder and ideological head of Hamas, a quadriplegic from the age of twelve, and almost blind, was killed while leaving a mosque after early morning prayers in Gaza City on March 22, 2004, his wheelchair destroyed by a missile fired from a distant Israeli gunship overhead. Yassin was the worst of the worst. He had spent nine years of a life sentence in Israeli prisons before being released on demand of the Jordanians, after the Mossad botched an attempt to kill another Hamas leader, Khaled Mashal, on Jordanian soil. The only way Jordan could show it was not party to the scheme was to be furious, threaten to cut off relations, and demand Yassin's release. Jordan also demanded that the head of the Mossad himself, Danny Yatom, fly to Amman with the antidote for the poison the Mossad's agents had injected into Mashal's neck and remain there until the Hamas leader improved. Today Mashal lives happily in Damascus and Yatom still gets red in the face when reminded of the humiliation.

As part of his release, Yassin promised not to encourage terrorism anymore, specifically suicide bombings, but the moment he set foot back in Gaza, he was back at it. In early March a decision was made to assassinate him after he personally ordered two suicide bombers to infiltrate the Ashdod port and blow themselves up on specific targets of chemicals and fuels that together would have created a mega-explosion with massive consequences for the port, which handles 60 percent of Israel's shipping, and the city of Ashdod, with a population of over 200,000 people. The two terrorists were smuggled out of Gaza in a double-walled container and managed to infiltrate the port's perimeter but blew themselves up before they reached their targets. Still, ten people were killed. Given the nature of the attack and its very different scale, a decision was made that it was time for Yassin to join the many *shahids*, martyrs, he had sent to their deaths.

I was in Zurich on the morning Yassin was assassinated. The breakfast television shows spoke of an Israeli attack helicopter using a missile to kill a poor wheelchair-bound quadriplegic cleric on his way out of early morning prayers at the Gaza mosque without any reference at all as to why Israel had carried out the attack. This was not because the news channels are anti-Israel, as many claim, but because those reporting the story were never provided with Israel's reasons for killing the sheikh. Those responsible for the country's public diplomacy heard about the assassination from the morning news, and it took them till four in the afternoon to put a profile together of who the sheikh really was and why he was killed. By then the narrative was set.

In both cases, Jenin and Yassin, there was no cooperation between the military carrying out the mission, and the foreign ministry charged with explaining it. If vetted news correspondents had been embedded with Israeli forces going into the Jenin refugee camp, they would have been able to report on the extraordinary constraints the army was fighting under to minimize civilian casualties. And if the foreign office had been made privy to the Yassin assassination plans early enough, they could have prepared a damning dossier to be released at the same time the sheikh was killed, specifying the Ashdod attack and the dozens of other incidents of terror for which Yassin was personally responsible.

Charges that Israel is guilty of war crimes are not new. The Balkan wars and the Rwanda genocide made "war crimes" and "ethnic cleansing" words to be applied to any situation, like the loose use of the word "apartheid." In an act of audacious hypocrisy, Belgium, the European colonialist country responsible for the murder of millions in the Congo, Rwanda, and Burundi and for the pitiful state of these nations to this day, enacted a law that gave itself universal jurisdiction to prosecute persons for genocide, war crimes, and crimes against humanity in absentia. Israel and Belgium have no issues dividing them; if anything, the opposite is true: Belgium is Israel's fifth-largest arms supplier, and the diamond trade is thriving between the countries. But during the intifada, as a result of the cumulative effect of the Muhammad Dura incident, Jenin, Yassin, and the fast-growing Muslim population in the country, Israel was placed in the dock, accused of war crimes and acts against humanity, together with the most odious criminals in the world.

The security barrier also took its toll on Israel's image in the world. On several occasions the UN deemed the barrier illegal, and later the International Court of Justice in The Hague ruled the barrier infringed on the rights of the Palestinians, was contrary to Clause Four of the Geneva Conventions, and should be removed. The whole judicial process was a media circus.

It is not exactly clear when criticism of the country stopped being about its policies in the occupied territories and started being about Israel's legitimacy, its right to exist among the family of nations. It was probably Israel's 2008–2009 war in Gaza that brought all the clusters of accusation and anger against Israel's handling of the Palestinians into one massive campaign against the country's right to exist.

The Gaza war and the Internet combined into a potent force to de-legitimize Israel in every forum in every way. The de-legitimization made it impossible for Israeli spokespeople to express themselves without interruption, caused English courts to issue warrants for the arrest of Israeli politicians and officers involved in the handling of the war, and made it unsafe for Israelis to openly travel in Jordan and Egypt, and even in Europe. The degree of de-legitimization became such that in 2010 the United Jewish Federations of America, the overarching body of all U.S. Jewish communities, made fighting Israel's de-legitimization its number-one nondomestic cause, though the group had good reason domestically for doing so. The more vitriolic the hatred against Israel, the more vulnerable Jewish communities become abroad. A relative of mine in Melbourne, Australia, wrote me during the Gaza war that "Israel's actions in Gaza were making it impossible for him to live as a Jew in Melbourne," something I would have laughed at, had I not been in Australia at the start of the Lebanon war in 2006 and seen the wave of hatred against Jews both in the media and from Australia's very large Lebanese community.

Israel had thought very carefully about how it would conduct its war in Gaza. It knew the world would be watching and that even if Israel succeeded in keeping the press out of the area, there would always be somebody with a cell phone and satellite dish able to broadcast what was happening, or rather what they wanted the world to believe was happening, as had happened in Jenin. In Gaza, from a public diplomacy perspective, Israel did not have a chance. Hamas had dug deep into Gaza's civilian infrastructure. It had arms caches hidden under homes; its head-quarters was in the basement of the local hospital. The organization had placed mortars and rocket launchers in mosques, schools, and public facilities. The streets and sewers were booby-trapped. Hamas had prepared for the war carefully, knowing that eventually Israel would have to respond to the group's constant rocket attacks. If attacked, they understood they could not beat the Israelis, but they could extract a heavy price from Israel, es-pecially if they could get Israel to hold its fire in consideration of the civilians entrenched in the battle zone. The more media Hamas could bring to the scene, the more inhibited Israel would be in using disproportionate fire power against Hamas, or in pur-suing Hamas fighters deep into densely populated Gaza City, where the collateral damage to civilians and civilian infrastruc-ture would be immense.

Israel managed to keep the foreign media out, and by elec-tronic jamming and other means kept reporting from inside Gaza to a minimum during the three-week conflict. But once the veil of secrecy was lifted and the world saw the results of the campaign, even Israel's friends shuddered. The damage seemed near total, the rubble reminiscent of pictures from the Second World War. People were dazed, families had been ripped apart, and over a thousand people had been killed. Hamas's tactics of hiding behind civilians had not deterred Israel from unleashing a storm on the list of targets where Hamas had its weapons and stores. But it was not Hamas that paid the price, its fighters having withdrawn deep into the inner circles of Gaza City, but the people of Gaza, who yet again lost all.

As for Israel, at the start of the war the world supported the country, understanding that no sovereign state could live with 6,000 rockets being fired at it over a period of years, and 450,000 Israeli civilians living in constant fear of attack. But the world could not accept the damage inflicted on the Strip's civilian population, and Israel was at a loss to explain it adequately. The subsequent UN-inspired Goldstone Report was devastating in its accusations against Israel, again framing the state as guilty of war crimes and crimes against humanity, and tightening the noose around Israel's neck by another few notches. Many months after the Goldstone Report was tabled, Israel finally responded to its charges one by one, refuting many with photographic evidence and detailed, military-type reports. The response was a work to be admired in its detail and the clarity with which it explained why Goldstone was wrong. But it was too late. It was even too late when finally, on April 1, 2011, Goldstone published an article in the *Washington Post* in which he recanted some of his findings, specifically those that found Israel guilty of deliberately targeting civilians in the Gaza campaign. By then, three years after the fact, only Israelis and their supporters—those who needed no convincing of Israel's justice—remembered what he was talking about. All the world remembers are alleged Israeli atrocities the UN claims Israel committed during the war. Goldstone's partial recantation was important and brave. But Israel was damned.

Israel now spends an inordinate amount of money on fighting what it believes is a bad press. Entire Jewish organizations live off this problem. One is Camera, which has a team of people watching newspapers for any slip, any inaccuracy, in its reportage on Israel, and making sure the editor, reporter, publisher, owner, and advertisers know about it. The Israel Project has a budget of $7 million a year to poll people around the world on their attitudes toward Israel and develops messages to help make Israel's case. Israel 21c sends out bulletins on how clever Israeli scientists are and how the country helps the world become a better place. The American Jewish Committee, the American Jewish Congress, the American Israel Public Affairs Committee, AIPAC, and the Anti-Defamation League all bring journalists and study missions to Israel to prove we are not monsters. The Israel foreign ministry spends millions on information campaigns abroad, until recently trying to rebrand Israel as a wine, cheese, and olive oil capital of the world. In 2008 the Netanyahu government established the Ministry of Information, which has wasted many millions on trying to convince Israeli travelers abroad to act as the country's goodwill ambassadors, giving them booklets at the airport that provide facts and figures proving what a wonderful country Israel is. "Did you know that Israel invented the cherry tomato?" the book asks. "Be sure to tell people. It will really make a difference." Sure.

Because it has been so successful, the campaign to discredit Israel and deem it illegitimate will continue even if Israel manages to come to terms with the Palestinians on the West Bank. The reality is that Israel will continue to have to take into account another war with Hezbollah and Hamas at some time in the future. That war will be fought, again, in heavily populated areas against an enemy embedded in civilian infrastructure. Israel can again phone families and drop leaflets in areas to be attacked in the hope that civilians will leave, but there will be civilian casualties and the pictures will be ugly. Israeli military intelligence can learn to release intelligence in real time that will help explain to the world why hospitals and schools are being attacked, but this will hardly help Israel's image as a quality purveyor of wine, cheese, and olive oil.

Israel should not be fighting for its legitimacy. It has long been legitimate, a lot more so than many of the regimes that sit in judgment of Israel. It would be easy for Israel to say to the NATO countries, "Look what you did in the Balkans, killing dozens of innocent civilians, destroying the Chinese Embassy by 'mistake,' leaving no stone unturned in the destruction of Kosovo." Or to turn on the Chinese with their human rights record, to confront the Russians on how they deal with terrorism from Chechnya and journalists who dare publish freely, or even to point fingers at the Americans with Guantanamo, and the United States and its allies embroiled in Afghanistan, where not a day goes by without civilian casualties and collateral damage being inflicted on people whose suffering is at least as tragic as that of the Palestinians in Gaza.

But Israel should not have to defend itself by pointing to the behavior of others. Nor should it take solace in the fact that of all the countries in the world only Israel was under boycott by British academics, and that some of its ministers and generals were at risk of immediate arrest if they landed on British soil, including the head of the Israeli opposition, Tzipi Livni, who happened to be Israeli foreign minister during Operation Cast Lead, as Israel termed the war in Gaza. Israel's social affairs minister, Yitzhak "Bougie" Herzog, son of a former president of the state, grandson of the first chief rabbi of Israel, and member of one of the most respected families in the land, canceled a trip to speak to British WIZO, the Women's International Zionist Organization, in the spring of 2010. He feared arrest under Britain's law that empowered local magistrates to issue warrants against suspected war criminals, a law never used until Israel became an object of such charges, no matter how thin and fallacious.

De-legitimization is the new tool the Palestinians and their supporters have found to hurt Israel. The Internet has made it easier, while the UN has given legitimacy to even the most outrageous claims against the country. On campuses around the world, efficient provocateurs have managed to make it difficult for Israelis to express themselves openly. Shimon Peres, the country's president who more than anyone else symbolizes Israel's desire for peace, was booed and heckled at the usually civilized Oxford University in 2008, an unprecedented occurrence in that forum. The Israeli deputy ambassador had to flee under a hail of abuse from a campus in Manchester, England, where she was scheduled to give a speech. Israeli prime ministers have been booed in even the friendliest of forums, as Binyamin Netanyahu was at the annual Jewish General Assembly in New Orleans, Louisiana, in 2010. I was verbally attacked while speaking at Berkeley in California by a Jewish group called Not in My Name, who seem to object automatically to almost everything Israel does, and yelled at me about everything from "apartheid walls" to "Nazis" and "children killers." It is easy to understand youths on campus taking up the cause of those they see as the underdog. It was once Israel they were rooting for. But it becomes serious when the university academic staffs, themselves teachers, impose a boycott on their Israeli peers, including world-renowned experts in their fields. It becomes serious when labor unions around the world join the academics, refusing to handle Israeli produce, and universities and churches start divesting their pension funds from Israeli stocks. It becomes serious when companies face boycotts if they invest in Israel, and Israel's bilateral relations with the world are constantly clouded by charges of criminal behavior. It is serious if Israel is placed in the same category as those countries where atrocities have been committed and where they are taking place now. Between 1,200 and 1,400 Palestinians died in thirty-three days of war in Gaza, while the civilian population was kept hostage on the battlefield by Hamas. In planning sessions before the war, it was thought that the number could have been ten times that. Before attacking targets in Gaza, Israel phoned residents and told them they had a few hours to leave their homes. No other army in the world has done that. And when Hamas forced entire families to stand on the roofs of their homes to protect the arms caches and bunkers beneath, Israel refrained from bombing the targets. It was an ugly war. What is there to say?

Israel does not have to defend itself to the world. To be open about it, the world has quite some explaining to do to Israel. Under the most difficult of circumstances Israel has remained a democracy when it very easily could have evoked the British Emergency Regulations of the mandate period, which remain on the books and enable the imposition of martial law. It remains a country of law, accountability, freedom of expression, political freedom, and deep liberal values. Most of the "dirt" brought to the public's attention on abuses of power, corruption, inappropriate behavior, and military excesses is done so by either the Israeli media or the many Israeli NGO watchdogs that monitor human rights in the occupied territories, the behavior of Israeli troops, and the conduct of government. When there are transgressions, Israeli courts deal with the problems. They have changed the course of the security barrier and sent Israeli government ministers to jail; they have forced the resignation of generals and sent prime ministers packing. Between the Israeli judiciary, the military judicial system, the state comptroller, and dozens of other avenues that are Israel's bulwark against moral turpitude in government and the security forces, the country does not need sanctimonious advice from the UN, one of the most self-indulgent organizations on the planet. No country has withstood the force of terror with more dignity than Israel.

Israeli occupation is not right. Its settlement policies are not right. The behavior of fringe settler groups against the Palestinians and their land-grabbing activities are scandalous and criminal. Occupation corrupts and there are acts of corruption in the armed forces. The roadblocks the Palestinians have to navigate are demeaning and time-consuming, and soldiers lose more humanity the longer they are in service. Mistakes are made, civilians are killed, and even dumb mistakes are made, such as the decision to briefly use phosphorous bombs in an urban area during the

Gaza war. All these things are true, but I defy any army to fight an enemy like Hamas in the circumstances of Gaza and come out clean, or to have to impose an occupation on two million people and remain humane. These are the realities of Israel's life.

Israel and those well-meaning, but largely ineffectual, organizations that try to work on behalf of Israel's good name should save themselves the effort. Israel will not win the propaganda war by claiming that it invented cherry tomatoes and plants more trees per year than any other country in the world. It should have not ignored the claims against it in the International Court of Justice in The Hague, and it should have cooperated with the Goldstone Commission. The country has nothing to hide. Not cooperating looks like an admission of guilt. Cooperation means recognizing the legitimacy of the body undertaking the inquiry, sometimes a problem. But the cost of silence is greater than that of holding one's nose and diving into the mud.

Public diplomacy crises are never over in Israel. In the spring of 2010 a Turkish-led flotilla arrived to break Israel's naval blockade on Gaza, though Turkey and Israel were supposedly friendly, and Gaza was in the hands of Hamas, defined by many of Turkey's NATO allies as a terrorist organization. The lead ship, the *Marmara*, was heavily loaded with Turkish thugs, Syrian intelligence agents, Hamas operatives, and many international Palestinian supporters who thought they were doing the right thing. Israel decided to divert the ship to an Israeli port and not permit it to dock in Gaza. Israeli commandoes boarded the ship while still in international waters, and a battle ensued in which nine people on board were killed, leading to a major break in Israeli-Turkish relations. Here, too, instead of the army and the foreign ministry working hand in hand to resolve the crisis, the commando raid was undertaken with no thought as to how this was all going to play on the news—not very well, as it happened.

Instead of apologizing for the past, however, Israeli public diplomacy officials should be conditioning the world for the future: making the world understand now that if there is another war in Gaza or Lebanon, or both, the consequences will be ugly. There is no aesthetic or clinical way to deal with an enemy who operates from a civilian base and has no scruples about hiding behind women and children, using hospitals and schools as bases of operation. Hamas and Hezbollah have understood that whoever controls the media controls the battle.

The short-term goal of Hamas and Hezbollah is to dehumanize Israel and bring it down to their own level in the eyes of the world, to show Israel as a terrorist state with no regard for the rule of law or basic human rights. They seem to have succeeded in some places, including the UN and the International Court of Justice, and with academics and justices in Belgium and Britain, among others. Israel used brute strength in Gaza to overcome the dangers of booby traps, suicide bombers, and ambushes. It stopped short of destroying Hamas's infrastructure, embedded in Gaza City, because of the collateral damage this would have caused.

In the 2006 war in Lebanon, most of Israel's response was directed toward Hezbollah, but that was before Hezbollah played a central role in mainstream Lebanese politics. Today, with the Iranians and Syrians, Hezbollah controls the country and the country's army, making all of Lebanon a target for Israeli retaliation. A new war would be ugly even if Israel played strictly by the rules of international engagement. Since the Gaza war, legal officers have been attached to military units to ensure that no international codes are transgressed, army-operated video cameras record every action against accusations of wrongdoing, and millions have been spent by the state and its friends on public diplomacy efforts of one kind or another. Still, all this will not convince those who want to believe otherwise. If Israel, however, says up front what the consequences of another war will be and exactly what the end result will look like, the world will not be able to claim that it did not know. And perhaps instead of criticizing Israel so persistently, the UN and its relevant agencies should invest their energies and resources in conflict resolution, not fanning the flames of hatred and supporting a wall of lies.

For Israel to be fighting for its legitimacy is an insult. The country should stop dealing with the question.

* * *

It could be very different. In December 2010 Israel suffered a terrible fire on the Carmel hills close to Israel's third-largest city, Haifa. Five million trees were destroyed and forty-four people died, and much of a kibbutz, Beit Oren, which had survived wars and terror attacks, was left in smoldering ruins. The fire was thought to have been started accidentally by a teenage boy who had gone off to a copse of trees near his home in the Druze village of Usifiya to secretly smoke a narghile, a water pipe. Though already early December, deep into what was supposed to be winter, the country had hardly seen a drop of rain and the forests so carefully and lovingly planted over the years were as dry as tinder. Most of the trees were pine, the wood used to make matches.

This, together with strong, varying winds, resulted in an ecological disaster some estimate will take a generation to overcome.

Though Israel has one of the most sophisticated air forces in the world and has spent billions on home defenses in the form of shelters, warning systems, and emergency medical services, its ability to fight fires was woefully inept, with the country having one firefighter for every 8,500 people as opposed to four times the number of firefighters per capita in most parts of the civilized world. It also had no aerial firefighting capability, because the decision of which planes to buy was stuck in committee for over fifteen years while bureaucrats fought over which government ministry would foot the bill.

When the dimensions of the fire became clear, the prime minister, Netanyahu, sent out an urgent call for international help. The Bulgarians were the first to arrive, soon followed by the Cypriots and surprisingly the Turks, even though Israel and the Turkish government were on the brink of severing relations at the time. Within a day, aircraft from fourteen countries, including Russia, the UK, Switzerland, and Germany, and firefighters from Jordan and the Palestinian Authority were battling the flames. Suddenly it seemed as if the entire world was trying to save the country vilified in Durban and onward, flying hundreds of sorties with as many as forty aircraft in the air at one time, under the command of an Israeli air force unit set up in Haifa to coordinate the effort. When it was over, the crews, some of whom had not slept for three or four nights, celebrated together, a common enemy defeated and the rhetoric of hatred left in the past, for the time being, at least. More important, as a result of the incident, the countries involved decided to create a regional rapid-response team to deal with similar tragedies in the future. It took a fire in Israel to get Greece and Turkey to work together, and the lesson has been learned. Greece, Turkey, Israel, and other Mediterranean countries share the same problem; now they are part of the same solution. While Israel's firefighting force was an embarrassment, some of the fire trucks being forty years old, it excelled in dealing with the crisis once the fire got started, with controllers vectoring pilots from all manner of countries into action, impressive coordination taking place between ambulance, ground, and air forces, and generally providing a model of organization and calm professionalism while the emergency lasted. The country has had a lot of experience with suicide bombings and other attacks, and the way it responds could be a model for others.

At the time of the fire, I was abroad at a second-track conference, this one also attended by colleagues from the Arab world. Among the subjects discussed were the implications of the significant natural gas deposits Israel has discovered some two hundred kilometers off the northern part of its coast, opposite Haifa. To date, the finds are enough to supply Israel's energy needs for many years to come and even allow for some exports, a true and major revolution for a country once almost totally dependent on energy imports. Early but reliable data from another discovery at the Leviathan field some two hundred kilometers offshore and even more to the north promise trillions more cubic meters of gas when developed. Both finds and subsequent geological data indicate that the reserves may extend well beyond Israeli territorial waters and into huge subterranean reservoirs in Lebanese territorial waters. Energy is one of Lebanon's most serious problems and the main reason for its budget deficit. A gas find would be a godsend for the country both economically and in terms of sovereignty and independence. But unlike Israel, which was quick to find international partners and put together a consortium that could act on geological presumption, the Lebanese have done nothing. Their government is ineffectual and weak. National projects are handled by a small clutch of elite families and Hezbollah, the real power in the land. Hezbollah has already started accusing Israel of stealing Lebanese gas, and instead of the massive potential benefits both countries could derive from the find, because of Lebanese governmental weakness and Hezbollah's lust for war, the gift may well turn into a curse.

Israel has much to offer in many fields. It could play a major role in solving world hunger. It has developed tomatoes and peppers that grow in salt water and wheat crops that produce higher yields. The country has developed irrigation methods that have brought about water revolutions in many countries and come up with the idea of mixing 30 percent recycled tires into the tar it uses on its roads, making them quieter and skid-proof. When Haiti had its terrible earthquake, the Israeli medical response made the world sit up and watch, and its medical electronics and contribution to the life sciences has been significant in many, many fields. To positively project Israel, a Web site, Israel 21c, sends out a weekly newsletter stacked with new Israeli inventions and ideas in countless fields, from a new anti-snoring device to breakthroughs in the early detection of breast cancer. Another indicator of what is to be found is the number of start-ups bought by international corporate giants each year, creating a whole new level of young Israeli wealthy who are the engine behind Tel Aviv's being voted the third-hippest city in the world by the Lonely Planet travel resource.

Far from Tel Aviv is Hatzeva, a *moshav*, cooperative farm, in the Arava, an arid wasteland in the south of Israel. When it was founded in the very early 1970s, those sent there were treated like national heroes off to achieve Ben Gurion's dream of making the desert bloom, but with no real hope of being economically independent, let alone prosperous. It was one of five such settlements set up at a junction some one hundred kilometers north of Eilat and about the same distance south of any city of size. There is no freshwater to be had, only deep subterranean pools of highly saline water thought to be useless until scientists at the Volcani Institute of Agricultural Research near Rehovot discovered otherwise. They also learned how to use the region's barren, arid soil to produce year-round crops. Today there are fields of eggplants, onions, tomatoes, peppers, melons, squash, basil, mint, arugula, thyme, and rosemary. There are acres of tulips, sunflowers, gladiola, lilies, gerbera, lisianthus, delphinium, and digitalis. Most of the growth is in hothouses, where nonstinging bees pollinate the plants. Thai workers, in Israel on five-year contracts, pick the produce and pack it straight into containers destined for the biggest marketing chains in Europe and many countries in the Arab world. The flowers go directly to the Netherlands, where they go on international auction in Schiphol the next morning. If Israel can export tulips to the Netherlands from the Arava, imagine what it could do for Sudan and the rest of the starving world if the diplomats of hate and unreason were not so busy with defamation and turned their attention to what Israel could offer instead.

This can be vividly seen from the border between Israel and Jordan facing north, you find no fence other than the remains of a fallen barbed-wire roll on the earth. To the right is Jordan, arid and dry and unsettled, not a tree visible on the horizon. On the left is Hatzeva, with miles of hothouses glistening like the sea in the sunlight, and beyond them rows of date palms as far as the eye can see, massive trucks leaving with crates of perfect peppers for Sainsbury's, the premier British grocer.

Israel and Jordan have been at peace since October 1994. What logical reason could there be for the disparity between the two countries, and what better way to cement peace than sharing knowledge and know-how? Jordan is not laden with excess bounty, and water is one of its main problems. Yet the reality is that the Israeli side of the border from the Dead Sea almost all the way down to Eilat is an almost uninterrupted journey through productive and ingenuous solutions to the region's problems. On the Jordanian side exists little other than a road and a railway connecting the southern port of Akaba to the center of the country. Israel is considering a proposal to build a canal from the Dead Sea to the Red Sea, the Dead–Red Canal. The idea is to use the difference in elevation between the two, the Dead Sea being the lowest spot on earth, to produce energy that, among other things, would desalinate water, allowing for both agriculture and urban settlement. The project is not simple, and it has yet to be fully analyzed in terms of environmental impact. The concept is that the canal be an international project with Jordan and Israel as partners. They share the Dead Sea and the northern mouth of the Red Sea, the Arava delta, they both need water, and they both need to stop the encroachment of the desert. The countries have cooperated on fly and pest control and other health-related issues. More of this type of cooperation would only serve to cement peace and make it more impervious to outside influences.

Until peace is cemented, security remains an issue, and because of Israel the world is a safer place. A victim of hijacking, Israel created sky marshals and cockpit procedures that have made serious hijacking a thing of the past. Much of the airport security equipment used the world over on both passengers and baggage is derived from Israel. The country advises other nations on internal security, helps secure the Olympic Games and other major international events no matter where they are held, and trains antiterrorist forces from all over the world. Its sophisticated electronic fence on the Lebanese border has become a model for many others with similar concerns. It is, unfortunately, a world leader in dealing with disasters, providing emergency services and identifying bodies, skills that played a major part during the 2004 tsunami in the Indian Ocean, working mainly in Sri Lanka, a major critic of Israel's policies.

The problem with all this, of course, is politics. Israel could be a light unto the nations if the nations would allow it to happen. It could help push the desert back and feed a hungry world, and contribute in medicine and space, alternate energy and water conservation. Israel is already deeply involved with India and China, two nations that for a long time did not recognize the country. Both giants have come here to find solutions to their needs and have a healthy respect for their Israeli counterparts, so much so that it can become an embarrassment. In 2005 an Israeli diplomat ended her four-year term at the Israeli embassy in Beijing. At a farewell party in her honor, her Chinese counterpart presented the Israeli diplomat with a beautiful leather-bound copy, in Chinese, of the *Protocols of the Elders of Zion*, one of the most heinous anti-Semitic texts ever written and inspiration for the slaughter of Jews from the time of the Cossacks to Hitler. Handing the departing diplomat the book, the Chinese foreign ministry official said that the book had provided her with a great lesson, that she admired the Jews and hoped China would achieve the same degree of world control, specifically over the banks and media, like the Jews had.

Another case, however, is the sorry story of an Israeli team of doctors dispatched to the Maldives by the Israeli foreign ministry in December 2010 to try to help control eye disease. There were hopes this would shore up Israel's diplomatic relations with the Maldives, an island nation of 300,000 people in the Laccadive Sea of the Indian Ocean, seven hundred miles south of Sri Lanka, the smallest nation in Asia and the world's smallest Muslim nation, and as far away from the Israel-Palestinian conflict as could be. Yet when the doctors arrived in Male, the capital, they were besieged by protestors claiming that Israel was there to do what Jews were known to do, especially to Palestinian children: steal their organs. The protests were stirred by the Islamic opposition movement, and President Mohamed Nasheed was quick to apologize. Patients still lined up for treatment, but the story led the Maldivian press and for days the "Israeli organ snatchers," not the work they were doing with hundreds of patients who needed their attention, became the talk of the day.

Israel's relations with the world could be very different if and when the country gets the Palestinian issue off the table. Sir Richard Branson, the British billionaire and entrepreneur, owner of the Virgin brand and pioneer of commercial space travel, gave an interview to Israeli television in November 2010 in which he said he loved Israel, would always support it, had high regard for its scientists and industrialists and for its entrepreneurial spirit, but that he would not invest in the country until there was peace. One could argue, however, that if he really supported peace he would invest in both Israel and the Palestinians, giving them both something to lose through continued conflict. Then again, the coin has two sides and could fall either way.

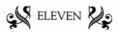

ELEVEN

Red, Blue, and White

Key to Israel's survival is its relationship with the United States. It is so central that many have called Israel the fifty-first state. America is critical to Israel's deterrence, and Israel's military would not be the fighting force it is if it were not for American arms sales, financial support, and technology sharing. The United States is Israel's guardian angel. It stands up for Israel at the UN and other hostile international platforms, has a strong influence over Europe's attitude toward Israel, and has shielded Israel from boycotts, embargoes, and other hurtful actions. Over the years America has dispensed tens of billions of dollars in aid to Israel, some of it direct, other in less tangible forms, such as scientific cooperation, research grants, refugee assistance, and military aid by other means, like pre-positioning American stockpiles in Israel, so that Israel does not have to buy its own. Just the intelligence America provides Israel is worth hundreds of millions of dollars a year.

The relationship between the two has had its ups and downs, sometimes even reaching crisis point, but has essentially always been solid. There was a crisis with the Eisenhower administration in October 1956 when Israel, together with Britain and France, launched the Sinai campaign in response to Nasser's nationalization of the Suez Canal, and again in the early 1960s, when the Kennedy administration discovered that a "textile plant" near Dimona was an Israeli nuclear reactor with bomb-making capacity. It was only after fractious negotiation and threats that Israel and America agreed to disagree and came up with the concept of "nuclear ambiguity," a policy that left Israel with the bomb and off-limits to international inspection. Another dark mark on the relations was the attack by Israeli pilots on a U.S. spy ship, the USS *Liberty*, in the opening phase of the 1967 Six-Day War. The Americans eventually accepted Israel's explanation that the attack was a case of mistaken identity—the Israelis thought the ship was an Egyptian destroyer, the *Ibrahim el Awal*. The incident, however, has been kept alive in hate form by a group of former crew members convinced that the attack was deliberate. Another dark period was the 1975 "reassessment" of the Ford administration, where arms transfers to Israel were suspended, including essential spare parts for the country's Phantom jets, because Israel would not commit itself to withdrawing from two strategic passes in the Sinai, the Gidi and the Mitle. The Reagan administration did not take kindly to the bombing of the Iraqi nuclear reactor at Osirak in June 1981, America being closely allied with Iraq in its war against Iran, with tension rising after Israel's invasion of Lebanon a year later. A terrorist attack in October 1983 on soldiers from a multinational force dispatched to Lebanon cost the lives of 241 American soldiers, mainly Marines.

Perhaps the most serious altercation between America and Israel came with the Jonathan Pollard affair. Pollard, a naval civilian intelligence analyst, started spying for Israel in 1984, providing the country with thousands of copies of top-secret documents, mainly pertaining to Iraq and other countries in the Middle East. In 1987 Pollard was sentenced to life without parole, and though several Israeli prime ministers have asked that he be pardoned, no American president—not even Bill Clinton, who was extremely close to Israel—has agreed. When Clinton was tending toward agreement, the head of the CIA at the time, George Tenet, threatened to resign. In December 2010 Binyamin Netanyahu wrote Barack Obama a formal and open letter for Pollard's release, citing Pollard's declining health. Previous requests were made quietly or as part of an overall diplomatic package. This was the first time Netanyahu had asked for Pollard's release openly and independent of any other consideration.

On top of Osirak, the Lebanese war, and Israel's intransigence on the peace process with the Palestinians, the Pollard affair threatened to alienate, not only the administration, but also the career defense community, with which Israel had always enjoyed close security ties cemented by common foes and mutual trust. The affair deeply embarrassed the Jewish community, particularly those Jewish activists on Capitol Hill who had spent their professional careers arguing that Israel was an ally of the United States. It cast a deep shadow of suspicion over Jews with sensitive jobs in government. It was an unforgiveable act of stupidity. Israel was receiving billions of dollars in aid; America shared intelligence with Israel as it did with NATO countries, and more so. No matter what Pollard passed along, it could not have been worth the damage caused.

Israel and America have always been at loggerheads over Israel's settlement policies. Israel's preoccupation with perennial coalition difficulties, where domestic politics take precedence over strategic issues, was also a source of great frustration to many in various American administrations. Henry Kissinger is famous for saying that "Israel has no foreign policy, only a domestic one." President Clinton used a four-letter expletive more than once at the Wye River Plantation talks between Netanyahu and Arafat in 1998, frustrated and angry over the Israeli leader's vacillations. Sometimes America's political leaders have sounded overly hostile; President Jimmy Carter referred to Israel as a "cancer" and later as an "apartheid state," making no effort to hide his disdain for the country. His national security adviser, Zbigniew Brzezinski, was considered Rasputin in Israel, and seen as an anti-Semite. Caspar Weinberger, President Ronald Reagan's secretary of defense, was the only foreign dignitary in the history of Israel to refuse to visit Yad Vashem, the memorial to the six million Holocaust victims. As for Richard Nixon, as the secret White House tapes released in December 2010 make clear, the president had no love for Jews. What came as a real shock when the tapes were released were statements made by Kissinger, the head of the National Security Council at the time, himself a Jew. He was recorded saying the Jews in the former Soviet Union could all be gassed: "The emigration of Jews from the Soviet Union is not an objective of American Foreign policy. If they put Jews into gas chambers in the Soviet Union it is not an American concern, maybe a humanitarian concern." To this Nixon replied, "I know we can't blow up the world because of this."

The conversation took place in March 1973, shortly after Israel's prime minister, Golda Meir, had pleaded for the right of

Jews to escape persecution in the former Soviet Union and to allow them to immigrate to Israel.

It is hard to understand how Kissinger, himself a Jewish refugee from Hitler's Germany who came to America as a boy of fifteen in 1938, could even think of Soviet Jews going to the gas chamber with such cold equanimity, but such was the language of realpolitik. Neither he nor the president would jeopardize American interests for Soviet Jewry, even if the Jews were in danger of physical annihilation.

Golda Meir was not alone in her plea for the release of Soviet Jewry. There was an extremely strong lobby in the United States as well, with Henry "Scoop" Jackson, the veteran senator from Washington state, leading the fight. But as the released fly-on-the-wall tapes so vividly reveal, when it comes to America's broader interests, the power of the Jewish community and Israel is severely limited. This does not diminish the importance of the Jewish community or its involvement in American politics on Israel's behalf. As long as Israel is a strategic asset and not an impediment, it will have America's support. When it hires Jonathan Pollard as a spy, or continues Jewish settlement on the West Bank or in East Jerusalem, despite specific assurances to the contrary, there will be trouble. Jewish political influence may be able to ameliorate the situation, but it will not be able to fundamentally change America's primary policy objectives. Despite the support and friendship, Israel has to tread a careful line. Israel also has to take into account America's changed relationship with the Arabs. When the United States was fighting Saddam Hussein in 1990, though Israel was considered America's strongest regional ally, it was told by the first Bush administration to stay out of the war completely. Bush had put together an Arab coalition against

Saddam's Iraq that gave America legitimacy for acting in the region. Israeli participation in the war would have jeopardized the Arab coalition. Syrians could hardly be seen fighting the Iraqis shoulder to shoulder with the Israelis. During the war Israel was attacked by Iraqi missiles, and the army was pressing for a response. Prime Minister Yitzhak Shamir sat tight. Though he had played games with the Bush administration on settlements, he knew better than to get in the way of American strategic interests on the global stage.

The reasons for Israel's special relationship with America are many, including guilt over the Holocaust, where America did little to stop the slaughter in the camps or to receive refugees from Hitler's ovens. In one incident in June 1939, the *St. Louis*, a ship carrying 937 refugees fleeing the Nazis, was refused permission to dock in the United States and asylum denied its passengers, who were sent back to Germany to "survive" under Nazi rule. It is no accident that the U.S. Holocaust Memorial Museum in Washington, D.C., is dedicated to the hope that America will not allow another Holocaust to happen, unlike during the Second World War. Though those who knew the Holocaust and feel the guilt, particularly the American Jewish community, are dying out, the memory remains through literature and education and national museums like the Holocaust Museum, and for many Israel is seen as history's antidote to Hitler's intentions. The constant peril Israel finds itself in, particularly from some of the same people who now threaten America, brings the specter of the Holocaust back, which in turn translates into natural empathy for the Jewish state.

Some tend to make light that Israel is the only democracy in the Middle East, but it is seemingly taken very seriously by the

American people, who have shed so much blood in defending democracy. At least in Israel's case, the blood in defending democracy is its own. Israel's democracy is constantly under threat from many directions, but it would be very easy to slip into martial law every time the country faced a security crisis. President George W. Bush danced on the edges of doing so after 9/11 with wiretaps, the Patriot Act, and Guantanamo. That Israel has remained a strong democracy despite many of its own 9/11s earns, I believe, the respect of many in the United States, particularly those who are the bastions of democracy on the Hill and in the media. The American media are often critical of Israel, particularly its settlement policies, abuses in the occupied territories, and discrimination against Israeli Arabs. Many critics, such as Tom Friedman of the *New York Times*, ultimately chide Israel for Israel's own sake, sort of like trying to get an errant younger brother back on track.

There are other deep fonts of support, particularly the Christian fundamentalists who are more Zionist than Herzl and are absolutely against Israel's making any compromises with the "heathens" over Judea and Samaria, let alone Jerusalem. This has less to do with Israel as a Jewish state and more with it not being a Muslim one; the Jews are seen as fulfilling the prophecies by wresting the holy land from the hands of the "infidels," thus heralding Armageddon and the "second coming." Post-Holocaust history for these sizable and politically important groups is proof of the validity of written biblical texts. The Holocaust and the creation of the state of Israel conform almost perfectly with Ezekiel's prophecies, as does so much else in the Bible and contemporary history. Though tremendously important for Israel at the American domestic political level, Christian support leaves many in

Israel suspicious, fearful of attempts to proselytize among the new immigrants from the former Soviet Union and groups like Jews for Jesus who have made a concerted effort to convert secular Israeli youngsters to Christianity. There is also the feeling that the fundamentalists are prepared to fight the Muslim infidels to the last drop of Jewish blood on the road to Armageddon, but once they get there it will be Jewish heads on the block again, as has happened so often in history. Pastor John Hagee, for example, the evangelical founder of Christians United for Israel, believes the Holocaust was part of a divine plan that came about because of Jewish disobedience. He writes that Hitler was from a line of "accursed, genocidally murderous, half-breed Jews" and calls liberal Jews "poisoned" and "spiritually blind." Yet Hagee is one of Israel's biggest supporters, almost blindly so. At last count he had been to Israel twenty-two times, bringing with him thousands of pilgrims who returned more Zionist than ever, without the slightest shadow of doubt in their minds as to whose land so-called Palestine is. Hagee has given millions of dollars to help Israel absorb immigrants from the former Soviet Union, and the sports and recreational center in the West Bank town of Ariel carries his name. He has received honors and awards from Israel and from Jewish institutions in America. Though most Jews and Israelis are less than comfortable with Hagee and those like him, when they see the tour buses empty out at hotels even at the worst of times, like during the intifada, and hear that he broadcasts on 8 networks and 160 television and 50 radio stations to a worldwide audience of around 100 million people, always putting Israel's case first in an age of de-legitimization, they put their discomfort aside. Better to have him as a supporter than an enemy, of which Israel, even in America, has more than enough.

According to ongoing polling by the Israel Project, based in Washington, D.C., and credited with a high degree of professionalism, rank-and-file support for Israel has actually grown over the years despite the anger of administrations over Israel's settlement policies. This could be attributed to 9/11, American horror over the way the Taliban treat women and one another, Jihadist terror, Saudi funding for Al-Qaeda, being held hostage to Arab oil and OPEC's prices, the duplicity of Pakistan, and many other negative examples. But as the data show, there is also a healthy respect for Israel that goes way deeper than problems with Islam, support that derives from positive reasons rather than fear and bigotry, which ultimately makes for a healthier relationship.

At the heart of it all, however, is the American Jewish community, without whose active involvement on Israel's behalf the strategic relationship between the two countries would be vastly different.

There is great concern in America that the Jewish community is diminishing through intermarriage, disinterest, lack of identification with Israel, and religious disenchantment. This may be so. Unlike Israel where Orthodoxy rules, in America most Jews are nonorthodox, being Reform, Conservative, and various shades of each. In Israel one has to be of a Jewish mother or converted, according to the stringent rules of Orthodoxy, to be Jewish. In America the definition of who is a Jew is less rigid, more liberal, and not uniform. The difference in interpretations is a source of deep resentment between the Israeli religious establishment and the American Jewish community, but also a nightmare for American Jewish demographers who are trying to work out the size of the community. The question remains: Does intermarriage bring more Jews into the fold, or do those marrying out give up their faith and identification? What happens to their children? How does one count?

Whatever the real numbers, the American Jewish community is acutely aware of the problem and is investing much in trying to correct the slide. There remains a strong core group of leadership in the community that is unique in many ways, with some of those most concerned about the future of American Jewry, such as the philanthropist Michael Steinhardt, defining themselves as atheists. Steinhardt, who created the Foundation for Jewish Life and acts as its chairman, together with another Jewish philanthropist, Charles Bronfman, founded Taglit-Birthright, which by the end of 2010 had brought over a quarter of a million young Jews from around the world for a ten-day emotionally and educationally packed free trip to Israel, and continues to do so at the rate of 37,000 per year, 70 percent of them from America. These young people, between ages eighteen and twenty-six, go on to become Israel's best ambassadors on campus and, thanks to the Internet and Facebook, maintain relationships that become meaningful later on. At first the program was met with great skepticism. Israelis, who pick up about a third of the tab for the program, felt it somewhat absurd to be paying for rich kids from America to come and have a good time in Israel for no cost at all, when Israeli schools and academic institutions are so underfunded. American Jewish organizations felt the money could be better spent at the community level, that the program was wasteful and not educational enough, ten days being just a flash in a lifetime experience. But the naysayers have been proven wrong. In the decade the program has been in operation, the results have been uncontested in terms of the contribution to Jewish identity and the personal relationships that develop as a result, acting as glue tying the Jewish world together and giving a sense of purpose and unity to the American Jewish community in particular.

There are dozens, if not hundreds, of similar programs, though far less dramatic and not as high-profile as Birthright. There are university exchanges, trips to Israel by high schools, Jewish Federations, temples, and synagogues, and exchanges between Jewish camps and those in Israel. There are cultural exchanges, programs with internationally renowned Jewish musicians running master classes in Israeli academies and vice versa, there are sport exchanges and the Maccabi Games, the Jewish Olympics. Jewish communities across America hold Israel expo days on Israeli Independence Day. There are religious trips and archaeological expeditions, and every Reform rabbi has to spend a year studying in Jerusalem. The Jewish Agency alone has dozens of programs with American Jewry, the agency now interestingly having moved its primary focus from trying to convince American Jews to move to Israel, to helping them remain Jewish in America. The strands connecting Israel and the American Jewish community are so numerous and diverse that it is hard to begin to describe them. For some the association with Israel is useful in terms of fundraising, Israel's problems being "sexier" than those of the Jewish Community Center of Greater Pittsburgh, for example. For others it is critical to their identity. But for most it is a sense of partnership, of having a stake in building a home for the Jewish people, and showing that the slogan "We Are One," which the Jewish Federations once adopted, happens to be true—perhaps more than most people know and understand. The scope of Jewish philanthropy in Israel is stunning, the money coming in, not only to help Israel with national projects, but also for education, enrichment, geriatrics, environment, the arts, and the building of national institutions, such as the Knesset, the Israel Museum, and the High Court of Justice. Family foundations and Jewish philanthropy have helped establish Israel's hospitals, universities, museums, and civil rights movement, progressive Judaism, and the fight for a green, clean Israel. They provide educational programs to the periphery and educational and cultural enrichment to soldiers. They have built the magnificent Jerusalem promenade and the Tel Aviv seafront and opera house. There is not a student in this country who has not sat on a bench, in a classroom, next to a vestibule, in a building, on a square, or on a campus named after some prominent Jewish family from the Diaspora.

For years now Jewish philanthropy has contributed directly to the quality of life in Israel, making it a good place to live despite the objective problems it faces. This is an immeasurable contribution to the country's viability. Israel cannot take American Jews for granted, that is for sure. Its actions immediately affect how the community is seen and can cause outbreaks of anti-Semitism. The wars in Lebanon and Gaza, and the perception of Israel as a lawless neighborhood bully, have hurt Israel and the Jewish communities' standing among liberals. The imperiousness of Israel's religious establishment and lack of tolerance toward Reform and Conservative Jews has also taken its toll, as did ridiculous legislation proposed by the Netanyahu government for an oath of loyalty to the Jewish state for new Israeli citizens, an obvious poke at the Arabs.

But at the core the bond remains tight and largely consensual, with those worried about erosion working hard to prevent it. The relationship is one of partnership, with each side gaining and giving, and as long as that remains the case, it will remain essentially healthy. If Israel can resolve the Palestinian issue, it will become even healthier, much of the friction between Israel and American Jewry hinging on the repercussions of occupation, and the plight of the Palestinians finding sympathetic ears among the Jewish community, again particularly on campus.

Anyone interested in the strength of Israel's relationship with the American Jewish community who read John Mearsheimer and Steven Walt's book on AIPAC, the pro-Israel lobby in Washington, might think it was indecently close. The authors accuse the organization of having a "stranglehold on Congress" and a "distorted American foreign policy," their texts reading not unlike a modern American adaptation of the *Protocols of the Elders of Zion*. Both authors are Jewish.

AIPAC, the American Israel Public Affairs Committee, is an American organization that supports Israel, and not an Israeli organization manipulating the American political system. AIPAC does what the milk lobby and the arms lobby, the advocates of the defense industries, and those who support Pakistan and those who support awareness of climate change do. They try to influence Congress to support their causes, a system that is as old as American democracy itself.

As it happens, AIPAC is extremely effective, with a membership of 100,000, its own building in Washington, D.C., and an annual budget of over $70 million. It works professionally and systematically to identify potential legislators who support Israel, helps them gain election, and follows through with them while in Congress. AIPAC knows how the Hill works, who is who, and what committees are important. It has batteries of lawyers who understand legislation and which laws could work in Israel's favor, be it appropriations or defense contracts, help with settling refugees, or identifying research funds for green energy. The group lobbies the defense establishment, promoting understanding of Israel's strategic needs and fostering defense cooperation. It works with the administration and executive branch on issues that are of importance to Israel, including such sensitive subjects as Iran and strategic cooperation. It brings dozens of congressmen, congressional aides, journalists, and others to Israel, and hosts many Israeli speakers at its U.S. events. It holds an annual policy conference in Washington attended by some 5,000 people, including 1,000 students, at which all the top administration officials appear as well as almost the entire Congress. The organization celebrates Israel's ties with America, is open and for all to see, and is very far from the sinister cabal that Walt and Mearsheimer try to portray.

AIPAC tries to stay clear of Israeli domestic politics, having had tempestuous relations with some Israeli prime ministers in the past. Most notable was Yitzhak Rabin, who saw AIPAC as overly intrusive in Israel's business, specifically when it opposed American arms sales to Egypt in the mid-1970s, which Israel supported to block the Soviets. There have also been tensions over Israel's settlement policies, though AIPAC is generally thought to be a right-wing, conservative organization. It is, however, more dedicated to Israel's security than to Israel's territory and when settlement causes entanglement with the administration, AIPAC considers it counterproductive to Israel's best interests in America. Otherwise, AIPAC and Israel are generally two peas in a pod. Because the organization knows it is under the microscope, both

Israel and AIPAC tread carefully, taking care not to give enemies unnecessary ammunition. The Pollard affair rang a warning bell, as did Walt and Mearsheimer's book. There was a real scare when the Justice Department accused two top AIPAC officials, Steve Rosen and Keith Weissman, of passing classified information obtained from Lawrence Franklin, a U.S. analyst working in the Pentagon, on to the Israeli government in May 2005. The charges were later dropped, but not before AIPAC was thrown into temporary disarray and an ugly fight developed between the organization and Rosen, who sued for wrongful dismissal. There was also a hugely embarrassing incident in 1992, when a senior lay member of the organization, David Steiner, then AIPAC's president, was recorded boasting how he had squeezed then secretary of state James Baker out of billions of dollars on Israel's behalf, and how AIPAC would influence the incoming Clinton administration's choice of secretary of state. The recording was made by Haim Katz, a New York property developer who said he thought Steiner's characterization of AIPAC's power was unhealthy for the Jews.

The Israel lobby, however, goes way beyond AIPAC. There must be two dozen national Jewish organizations, from J-Street at the left end of the spectrum, to the Zionist Organization of America on the extreme right, all claiming to represent Israel in one way or another, in addition to their domestic agendas. There is the Anti-Defamation League and B'nai B'rith, the American Jewish Congress, and the American Jewish Committee, and at the very influential think-tank level the Washington Institute for Near East Policy, set up in the early 1980s to counter the anti-Israel sentiment coming from William Quandt at the Brookings

Institution, who was advocating a tough administration approach toward Israel at the time. A former member of the National Security Council in both the Nixon and Carter administrations, Quandt had been involved in brokering Israel's peace with Egypt and was convinced that only through pressure and sanctions could Israel be brought to the negotiating table with the Palestinians. Those at the Washington Institute, then headed by Martin Indyk, a former AIPAC staffer, later twice American ambassador to Israel, and senior State Department official in the Clinton administration, believed that the parties had to be nurtured into a peace process with confidence-building measures and proportionality, a step-by-step process, rather than a banging of heads. Indyk later went on to found the Saban Center at the Brookings Institution, ironically Quandt's old stomping ground. Sadly, the same issues the two were arguing about then are still being argued about now.

Binyamin Netanyahu's relations with the Obama administration started off on the wrong foot. Netanyahu would have preferred John McCain as president. McCain was a known quantity, a friend of Israel, and would be a continuation of the heady George W. Bush years, when it seemed Israel could do no wrong. McCain was also the obvious choice of Netanyahu's rich Republican friends, such as Sheldon Adelson, the gambling billionaire from Nevada, and Ron Lauder, the cosmetics heir, both staunch and generous Netanyahu supporters, who saw Obama as a threat to America's and Israel's national interests.

It seemed to those who watch these things in Israel that on taking office, though so many Jews were behind his campaign, Obama was off on a course that would be not only a departure from the Bush years but a radical one as well. The new U.S. approach to Iran would be one of negotiation, with conciliation being the new administration's catchword. The administration's primary focus was an orderly withdrawal from Iraq, and on Afghanistan, Pakistan, and Al-Qaeda. It was also decided to make it a priority to repair America's relations with the Muslim world, requiring an end to the Israel-Palestinian problem as quickly as possible. The Israel-Palestinian problem had become an irritant on a fragile stage of world problems. It also threatened America's alliances with the Arab world. In late 2010 WikiLeaks released cables quoting King Abdullah of Saudi Arabia urging Washington to "cut off the snake's head" while there was still time, referring to the Iranian nuclear program. America and Saudi Arabia also signed a $30 billion weapons deal in 2010, the Saudi way of helping to finance the war in Afghanistan. America has military presence in Kuwait, Qatar, Bahrain, and Yemen, and significant intelligence bases in Saudi Arabia and Jordan. The security of the Gulf is a primary American interest given the energy the United States imports from the region. These alliances are important to America in its war on terrorism, its bid to contain Iran, and its ability to support stability in emerging Iraq, and they also provide the United States with the pre-positioning of forces able to intervene deep into Iranian territory or wherever required. In terms of keeping alliances with the Arab world stable and forging ahead with detente with the Muslim world, the Israel-Palestinian conflict could only be a wild card with potentially damaging consequences for both goals.

A sign of this came in March 2010 from America's top soldier, General David Petraeus, the commander of American forces in Iraq and later Afghanistan, when he told the Senate Armed

Services Committee that "Arab anger over the Palestinian question limits the strength and depth of American partnerships with people" in the region. Earlier, David Axelrod, President Obama's senior adviser in the White House, said that ending the Israel-Palestinian conflict was "an imperative for American security."

Clear signs that Israel was in for a bumpy road came with President Obama's speech in Cairo in June 2009. Speaking at Cairo University, the event cosponsored by Al-Azhar University, a center of higher Islamic learning, he made his historic plea for a "new beginning" between America and the Muslim world. He repeated what he had said in Ankara in April of that year, that "America is not—and never will be—at war with Islam," and that American interests and those of Islam "overlap." He went on to say, to ever-mounting applause, that "America will not turn our back on the legitimate Palestinian aspiration for a state of their own" and "just as Israel's right to exist cannot be denied, neither can that of the Palestinians," and then the punch line: "The United States does not accept the legitimacy of continued Israeli settlements," drawing a line in the sand of America's relations with Israel in the Obama era. "This construction violates previous agreements and undermines efforts to achieve peace. It is time for these settlements to stop." He could not have been clearer, and his pledge to this specific audience could not have been more meaningful.

As part of the healing process between America and the Muslim world, he was saying, Israel would be kept on a short leash as part of the bargain. Israeli settlements on the West Bank and Jerusalem became the focal point of American foreign policy in the Near East, and if American-Muslim relations deteriorated, it would be because of some Israeli building project somewhere on the West Bank, even in long-established Jewish neighborhoods around Jerusalem, essentially within the consensus of what will remain in Israel at the end of the day.

In his speech, Obama also managed to upset many Jews when he alluded to equivalency between the Holocaust and the plight of the Palestinian people. "Six million Jews were killed—more than the entire Jewish population of Israel today. Denying that fact is baseless, ignorant, and hateful."

Then, after decrying anti-Semitism and those who would want to destroy Israel, he continued, "On the other hand, it is also undeniable that the Palestinian people—Muslims and Christians—have suffered in pursuit of a homeland. For more than sixty years they have endured the pain of dislocation." He ended: "So let there be no doubt: The situation for the Palestinian people is intolerable. America will not turn our backs on the legitimate Palestinian aspiration for dignity, opportunity, and a state of their own"—a statement that could be interpreted as meaning that Israel was directly responsible for all the problems of the Palestinian people and that Israel's actions were comparable to those of the Third Reich, in context if not in so many words. The president went on to condemn violence and told Hamas to mend its ways, but little of that was heard in Israel or among the American Jewish leadership. Warning bells were ringing all over the place and some people had a sinking feeling that the impossible was happening: America was abandoning its alliance with Israel and moving over to the Arabs. Obama had specifically rededicated America to Israel's defense in Cairo, but oil and the need to stabilize Iraq and Afghanistan were stronger than words, and the worst was expected.

The "worst" came in late March 2010, when Obama and Netanyahu met in Washington, where the American president went out of his way to humiliate Netanyahu. The president refused to have a photo opportunity with Netanyahu, something virtually unheard of and afforded to even the most odious of dictators who make it through the White House door, and then when Netanyahu refused to commit Israel to end construction, the president excused himself from the meeting, saying he was going to have dinner, telling Netanyahu if he needed anything to call. Scholars of modern American diplomacy were hard put to find a parallel incident on record.

The reason for the president's wrath was understandable. March had started off well and full of hope. George Mitchell, then the president's special envoy to the Middle East, announced on March 7 that the Israelis and Palestinians had finally agreed to proximity talks, after a year of not speaking and intensive diplomatic effort by the Americans to get both sides on track. In November 2009, after much arm-twisting, Netanyahu had finally agreed to Obama's demand for a settlement freeze, but only for ten months and not including East Jerusalem, which Israel claimed as its own, having annexed the territory in 1967. With Israel committed to a settlement freeze and the sides agreeing to talks, President Obama decided to send Vice President Joseph Biden to the region to bolster the sides and create goodwill. Biden vowed unyielding support for Israel's security and took a strident view on Iran, leaving a positive impression on his hosts, who, hours later, went on to humiliate the vice president, anger Obama, and leave those Palestinians wanting to see an erosion of American-Israel relations rubbing their hands in glee. Eli Yishai, Israel's interior minister, with Biden still in Jerusalem in the comfort of the presidential suite of the King David Hotel, announced plans for building 1,600 apartments for his constituents in the ultraorthodox neighborhood of Ramat Shlomo in East Jerusalem in territory the Palestinians claim as part of a future state. Needless to say, the fury in the administration was endless. Netanyahu spluttered excuses about not knowing this was going to happen; that Yishai was acting on his own; that this was a bureaucracy speaking, announcing the end of a three-year planning process without taking into account international implications. This all fell on deaf ears, already burning with anger. It was seen as a slap in the face, an attempt by Netanyahu to slip by his responsibilities and to play the president and the vice president for fools. The announcement turned a mission of goodwill and support into a huge embarrassment for the administration. They could not accept that the prime minister did not know that the building of 1,600 housing units was about to be announced, of all places, in contested East Jerusalem. For the president and his staff, it was proof of the worst they had been told about Netanyahu and his evasiveness, his inability to keep his word; a man of tricks and deviousness; a man who was not to be trusted.

It took a lot of corrective diplomacy before Netanyahu and the president met again in July 2010, much of the hard work being done by Secretary of State Hillary Clinton, Special Envoy Mitchell, and Dennis Ross, a veteran diplomat, former Middle East coordinator in the Clinton administration and now back in the State Department. The July 7 meeting, their fourth, was designed from the outset as a "new beginning" between the sides, albeit a less spectacular one than Obama's "new beginning" with the world of Islam in Cairo a few months before. This time hordes of photographers were invited in to record the smiling couple exchanging handshakes and pats on the shoulder and the meals provided by the White House with Obama and the First Lady playing graceful hosts to Netanyahu and his wife, Sara. At the July meeting Netanyahu let "drop" to reporters in the Oval Office that he wanted talks to resume with the Palestinians, this time directly. And Obama told the press that "the fact of the matter is that I have always trusted Prime Minister Netanyahu since I met him before I was elected president, and have said so publicly and privately," leaving Netanyahu glowing with satisfaction, almost as if he himself believed what he was hearing.

At the time of the meeting there were still several months till September 26, when the settlement freeze Netanyahu had agreed to ran out. Netanyahu had committed himself to a deal by 2012, which Obama thought worth recognizing. But no sooner had the Netanyahus packed their bags and left for Israel, the roller coaster in relations started again, this time with all American efforts focused on trying to extend the freeze, rather than letting the issue be resolved by speedy negotiation where America's real efforts should have been concentrated. As a result, the Palestinians decided to end all talks until Israel agreed to a total settlement freeze (why should they agree to less than the Americans were demanding?) and the Israeli nationalists found themselves with veto power over a possible peace settlement. The more Obama spoke about a freeze, the more he encouraged the nationalists to build. The Right realized that making provocative moves in Jerusalem by buying Arab property through straw companies, then creating a Jewish presence in the heart of Palestinian territory, was a way to stop talks that could end in Israel's having to give up most of the West Bank. The more the administration made settlements an issue, the more it could torpedo advancement on peace. Obama's concentration on the settlement freeze was a fundamental mistake and a recipe for disaster, and it was good only when it was taken off the table.

Strangely enough, during this entire period of rocky diplomatic relations, Israel's defense cooperation with the Americans could not have been better, brought to a point that Israeli defense officials say they have never been before. Hezbollah, Iran, Syria, Islamic Jihadist terror, and Hamas were all shared concerns. Turkey's swing toward Iran and Syria, along with growing anti-secular Islamic sentiment in the country, was also a common interest, as was the succession issue in Egypt, with President Hosni Mubarak being in his eighties and ill, and the impact of the massive influx of Iraqis into Jordan. There was also a deep American interest, as in the first Gulf War, in Israel's remaining on the sidelines, allowing the Americans to deal with its Arab and Islamic allies, along with the problems it faced. America did not want a repeat of the Osirak attack by Israel on the Iranians, or any unilateral action by Israel in the region. Israel's attack on the Syrian nuclear reactor, as we now definitely know from the WikiLeaks cables, was done in total collusion with the United States, Israel first asking President Bush to do the job and then getting a wink and a nod to do so itself.

Perhaps the most overt manifestation of the depth of the relationship was the announcement in October 2010 of a $2.75 billion deal between the United States and Israel for twenty F-35 stealth fighters, Israel being among the first countries in line for the advanced American aircraft, and the only nation to receive the plane without having invested in its massive development costs. Never before had the Americans sold Israel an advanced fighter so close to its development, the first prototypes of the F-35 having come off the assembly line only in 2008.

The supply of the F-35 to Israel goes way beyond the sale of an aircraft by one country to another. It entails the sharing of America's most advanced and closely guarded secret technologies. With the plane come avionics and electronics, communications, applied materials and radar, weapons systems, and ordnance. It brings to Israel's doorstep a whole new world of technology, described by one of my colleagues at the Institute for National Security Studies and on loan from the air force as a "quantum leap" from every point of view. To absorb and service the planes, Israeli air force personnel will be schooled in new levels of technology, and infrastructure will have to be upgraded and adapted and super-sophisticated communications systems integrated into the Israeli command structure. The aircraft brings with it an array of new munitions with new guidance systems and, importantly, it brings Israeli defense personnel into working relationships with the Americans and other international co-developers on the plane, which keeps them where they have to be to ensure Israel's security.

In other overt expressions of the alliance between the two countries in recent years, Israeli and American armed forces have conducted joint maneuvers at the strategic and tactical levels. Marines have trained at Israeli infantry bases in the Negev to prepare for Iraq, the terrain being similar, and American and Israeli pilots dogfight regularly. In October 2009 the United States and Israel held a three-week joint exercise code-named Juniper

Cobra, described by a security analyst for CNN as the "largest and most complex bilateral missile defense exercise to defend against attack from Iran ever held" and involving thousands of troops. A similar joint exercise was scheduled for 2011. Israel and the United States cooperated on a wide spectrum of weapons developments, from the Arrow anti-missile system to proximity triggers, and because of this cooperation Israel has had to cease lucrative arms sales to China—only after a nasty fight—because of what the Americans feared would be technology leakage to its competitor.

On Iran the cooperation between the sides is very, very close. There was a bump on this path in 2007, when the joint intelligence staffs issued a naive report that Iran had given up its nuclear research program. From then on, however, cooperation and intelligence sharing on Iran have reached new levels, and as much as can be ascertained, significant cooperation exists on the operational level as well in slowing down the Iranian program through sabotage and other means. The fact is that by the end of 2010, both American and Israeli analysts were seeing a slowdown in Iran's race toward an arsenal of nuclear weapons, plagued by all sorts of problems that neither country would claim as its doing, but did so with a certain smugness that made the disclaimer suspect. As 2011 came about, Mahmoud Ahmadinejad was faced with Sunni terror in northern Iran, with bread and fuel riots throughout the country as subsidies the government could no longer afford were being withdrawn; disquiet on campuses and the middle class; his top scientists being killed on the streets of Teheran or defecting to Mecca; and mysterious viruses attacking his computers and uranium-enriching centrifuges. This was a war

America, Israel, and others had decided to fight by other means, and the results were beginning to show.

What is known about this war, and much else about defense cooperation between Israel and the United States, is in indirect proportion to the depth of the relationship behind it. As long as Israel and America have common cause, the strong ties beneath the surface will remain strong despite stormy seas above. The strategic dimension of the relationship between the two is mutually beneficial, and that is why it has weathered even the worst of crises. It will remain so as long as Israel springs no major strategic unilateral surprises on the United States, and if Israel itself realizes that settlements are harmful to its own broader interests. It would be unforgivable to jeopardize the speedy supply of the F-35s by the administration and the "quantum leap" to Israel's security these aircraft bring with them if Israel, through its settlement policies, especially in East Jerusalem, made the country more of a bother than it is worth. The U.S. Air Force is waiting for 2,443 of the planes, already behind schedule, and an angry administration could easily move Israel to the back of the queue.

At the end of the day, America is America and Israel is Israel, and the latter is linked to the former by an umbilical cord. For America, Israel is just another leg on a centipede, necessary but not critical. Israel's policy makers would do well to remain aware of the difference even in the headiest of times.

 TWELVE

Jerusalem

Shalom, *salaam*, peace, is at the root of Jerusalem's name. Unfortunately, for most of its "recent" history, since it was founded by King David in 1000 BCE, the city has known anything but. It has been attacked and besieged over eighty times, captured and recaptured forty-four times, and destroyed twice. First came the Babylonians in 586 BCE, who destroyed the Temple of Solomon, took with them to Babylon those Jews they thought could be useful, and slaughtered the rest. Then came Persians, Greeks, Hasmoneans, Romans, Arabs, Crusaders, Tartars, Ayyubids, Mamlukes, Ottomans, British, Jordanians, and, finally, in 1967, modern Israel, which conquered the eastern half, with its historic sites, and claimed the city as its eternal, united, and undivided capital.

Jerusalem today is a beautiful, if troubled, city. Despite its many problems, it is a city of grace and magnificence, a beneficiary of wise principles set by the British in terms of its development outside the walls of the Old City during the mandate, and a driven effort by the Jewish state to reclaim Jerusalem as its own after unification in 1967. The British passed an ordinance that Jerusalem's new neighborhoods be built of Jerusalem stone, and British city planners and architects laid down neat roads and intersections they named after their kings and queens, generals and governors.

Until the turn of the nineteenth century, almost all of Jerusalem was contained within the walls of the Old City. Outside, on the biblical landscapes of Jerusalem's hills, monasteries took over massive tracts of land where Jerusalem's modern suburbs were to be built, making the churches the largest single landowners in the city and creating an anomaly whereby the official residence of Israel's president, the prime minister's residence, the chief rabbinate, the Jewish Agency, the courts, and even City Hall are on church land, leased out on long-term contracts in return for a tithe. The churches in question come from every shade of Christianity: Franciscan, Greek Orthodox, Red and White Russian Orthodox, Catholic, Anglican, Ethiopian, Copt, Armenian, and dozens of others, for whom the tithe is symbolic, but whose ownership of the land is not. The Israelis and Palestinians can decide what they may about Jerusalem's political future, but the land will continue to belong to the church.

Israel has gone to tremendous lengths to cement its hold over Jerusalem. It expanded the city limits into the West Bank, and since the early 1970s new neighborhoods have been built in either "no man's land" along the old border, or inside what used to be the West Bank, creating a ring of Jewish settlement around the city as if to encircle it from outside attack, a laager of sorts. The idea was to try to obliterate the line between east and west, between Arab and Jewish Jerusalem. In this Israel has been successful. By June 1993 the number of Jews in Arab East Jerusalem overtook the number of Arabs (155,000 to 150,000) and by early 2009 some 40 percent of the Jewish population of Jerusalem was living in neighborhoods on the Arab side of the 1967 Green Line, or in "no man's land," as a narrow strip between the sides was called in certain parts of the city where the borders were not contiguous.

Jerusalem is Israel's largest city and also its poorest. It is built on solid rock, making infrastructure installation like sewers and roads extremely expensive. Most of its inhabitants are either ultra-orthodox or Arabs, and both groups have more than twice the fertility rate of the rest of the country. Most ultraorthodox and Arabs live below the poverty line and depend on child support and other social benefits, and require massive outlays in health, education, and social services, many of these footed by the municipality. Due to high rates of intermarriage in both the ultra-orthodox and Arab communities for traditional reasons, there is also a higher rate of genetic medical problems that require special services. Jerusalem, for example, has the highest per capita incidence of Down syndrome in the OECD, the thirty-four-member international organization that measures growth in developed and developing countries. Jerusalem is also severely limited by the law that large families, which make up most of Jerusalem's population, and religious institutions, of which there are many in the city, pay no municipal taxes, so while the city enjoys revenue from the hundreds of absentee wealthy Jewish families from abroad who have luxury homes in the city, there is very little large business or industry in the city, and living off tourism is risky. One attack and the cancellations flow in.

Though the government offices, the Knesset, High Court of Justice, the Israel Museum and the Shrine of the Book, the Hebrew University, Yad Vashem, and Israel's other main symbols of nationhood are in Jerusalem, it is seen as a backwater. By the end of 2010 it did not even have regular train service to anywhere. The line in current use was built by the Ottomans in 1892 and is picturesque but totally inefficient. A new express line is promised by 2017, but skeptics say the Messiah will arrive first. The majority of Jerusalem's working population are either academics, civil servants, or in public service. Because yeshiva students are subsidized not to work, the number of unemployed people is inordinately high. The exodus of young secular or mildly religious educated and qualified people from Jerusalem over the years has reached plaguelike proportions. Good jobs are scarce; housing is expensive; and the growth of the ultraorthodox and Arab communities is vicelike and suffocating. As opposed to the sunshine and beaches of Tel Aviv and Israel's coast, Jerusalem is dour, tense, intolerant, and economically and culturally second-rate. Jerusalem is a place of little opportunity and limited options for the future.

There are those, of course, who see a different Jerusalem, a spiritual, mystical Jerusalem with the aura of the Old City, Temple Mount, Mount Zion, the Church of the Holy Sepulcher, the Mount of Olives opposite the sealed David's Gate in the walls of the Old City from where the Messiah will enter, and from where the dead will rise as in Ezekiel's prophecies. This is undoubtedly one of the most wondrous cities to explore, the finds endless, the history bottomless. But it's hard to take that to the bank. It has been, for better or worse, my home for forty-six years.

Despite its historical upheavals and the undeniable complexity of its demographics, politics, geography, and religious claims, Jerusalem is a lot more stable than usually assumed. Haram al-Sharif, the Temple Mount, has been in the hands of the Waqf since 1187, with the keys to the Mount in trust with the king of Jordan, who is also responsible for its upkeep. In 1992 he paid $8 million out of his own pocket for the 5,000 plates of gold it took to refurbish the Dome of the Rock. The Church of the Holy Sepulcher, built on the Hill of Calvary where Christ was crucified and buried in the southwest corner of the Old City, is a another example of long-term stability, impervious to the rages of politics going on around it. After the church was burned to the ground in 1853, the sultan used the opportunity to get the sides to sign a new agreement he called the "status quo to remain forever." To this day the site is shared by the Eastern Orthodox, Roman Catholic, Greek Orthodox, Coptic Orthodox, Armenian Apostolic, Ethiopian Orthodox, and Syriac Orthodox churches in relative harmony, though with some tensions, each knowing to the last flagstone and brick what is theirs and what is not.

From day one Israel made the very wise decision to freeze the status quo for all religions in conquered Jerusalem, and guaranteed both freedom of religion and access to the holy sites for all religions, something that had not been the same under King Hussein when Jordan controlled the Old City and East Jerusalem and allowed only very limited access to Christian sites, and no access at all to the Jews, not even to the Wailing Wall, literally a stone's throw away from the Jewish line. By ensuring religious freedom and respect for the holy sites and those who control them, Israel hoped to gain international legitimacy for its annexation of the city, an act that had been rejected by all and recognized by none.

Having smartly left the Haram al-Sharif in the hands of the Waqf and Jordan, and the churches secure with their own properties and rights, Israel went on to rebuild the Jewish quarter of the Old City that had been totally razed by the Jordanians, including thirty-three of its thirty-four synagogues, and to clear and broaden the section around the Wailing Wall itself. Fortunately for all, truly religious Jews will not ascend Temple Mount until the Third Temple is built, which could take some time, removing a potential source of trouble in the highly contended and sensitive area. There have been riots on Temple Mount over the years but they have not been with nationalistic Jews carrying Israeli flags and proclaiming the Mount in God's name, which has the potential to ignite riots against Israel and Jews the world over.

Not since Umar al-Khattab guaranteed the Monophysite Christian Church and its patriarch, Sophronius, that its churches would not be converted into mosques, as was the tradition of the time, has religion enjoyed as much freedom in Jerusalem. Nationalism, however, is another story, and an ugly one at that. It combines an unhealthy mix of history, religion, politics, real estate, rich Jews with Mad Hatter ideas, willing disciples who claim they know what God wants, corrupt lawyers, dubious Arab landowners, and a cabal of Israel officials at different levels who are dedicated to making Jerusalem Israel's undivided capital forever, by whatever means. These are people who for religious, security, and political reasons see no place for compromise and believe that all of

Jerusalem, including the most far-flung Palestinian village, should remain part of Israel's "eternal capital."

On November 23, 2010, a few religious Jewish settlers under heavy guard moved into a house in the Al-Farouk neighborhood of the village of Jabal Mukaber on the southeastern edge of the city, a hamlet of about four hundred Palestinian families, some of whom still have flocks of goats and a cow or two in their yards. There is nothing Jewish about Jabal Mukaber other than bad news, it being on the slopes of the Hill of Evil Counsel, where legend has it Judas gave up Jesus and the Pharisees sentenced Jesus to die on the cross. Today the Hill of Evil Counsel serves as the headquarters of the United Nations to the Middle East.

The organization behind the purchase of the house for its new Jewish tenants is called Elad, a high-profile right-wing and aggressive settler group led by a former Israeli commando officer, David Beeri, who worked underground in the occupied territories arresting terrorist suspects in the middle of the night. Elad has attracted big money from right-wing nationalists abroad, including some of the world's wealthiest Russian oligarchs, and its goal is to keep Jewish control over Jerusalem down to the last peripheral Arab village. Elad has also managed to gain control over the archaeological dig and tourist project at the City of David, and of much of the Holy Basin around the southern end of the Old City, which is hugely controversial and could ignite long-dormant religious conflicts, in addition to Jerusalem's national ones, if handled without sensitivity and skill.

The house bought from Arabs in the middle of Jabal Mukaber was purchased by a straw company called Lowell, whose Israeli representative was none other than David Beeri, the head of Elad.

The home had been bought from a Palestinian part-owner of the property who was dying and wanted to leave his family some money, which Elad happily paid him, though it is doubtful he had the right to sell the entire house, which had more than fifteen people living in it from three branches of the Karain family. After two years in Israeli courts it was decided the sale was legal, and families who had lived in the house for over thirty years were evicted with the world's press on their doorstep. A few hours later, with the media still there, armed guards escorted the new Jewish tenants into their new home in the middle of a dense Arab neighborhood with not a Jew in sight, but with an excellent view of the Old City and Temple Mount if they could see it past the barbed wire, wire mesh, and guard posts that surround their property.

Another settler group, almost in competition with Elad, is Ateret Cohanim. The group started in 1978 as a small yeshiva with eight students and is now a major facilitator for the purchase of Arab properties in the Muslim Quarter of the Old City and immediately outside it in suburbs like Silwan and Sheikh Jarrah, which they consider to have Jewish significance and should not be in the hands of Arabs.

Sheikh Jarrah is an Arab neighborhood on the road up to the Mount of Olives, one of the first Arab settlements outside the walls of the Old City in the 1870s, and the burial place of Shimon Hatzadik, Simeon the Righteous, the Jewish high priest at the time of the Second Temple who is credited with dissuading Alexander the Great from destroying Jerusalem. It has been a site of Jewish pilgrimage for Orthodox Jews in the past and is becoming more so as the battle for Sheikh Jarrah escalates.

By the turn of the twentieth century there were 117 Muslim, 97 Jewish, and 6 Christian families registered as living in Sheikh Jarrah. It was abandoned in 1948 and placed in the hands of the Jordanian Custodian of Enemy Property, which in 1956 allowed twenty-eight Muslim families to move into empty houses in the area, including Jewish-owned homes in Sheikh Jarrah. In 1967 the property reverted to the Israeli custodian, who held the property in trust for its owners, and who allowed the Arab families living there to remain.

Sleeping dogs were left to lie in the neighborhood until the mid-1980s, when Miami businessman Dr. Irving Moskowitz, with a lot of help from sympathetic municipal and government officials, bought the historic Shepherd's Hotel, not without a sense of historic justice, since it was once the villa of the much-hated mufti of Jerusalem, Hajj Amin al-Husseini, a loyal ally of Hitler. The issue languished for over twenty years, with Moskowitz finally winning court and municipal approval to go ahead in 2010 with development plans, despite the protestations of the Palestinians and descendants of Hajj Amin al-Husseini. In any other city this would have been a property dispute at most, but in Jerusalem in 2010 it had strategic consequences that stood at the heart of Israeli-American relations.

America was dead against any further Israeli settlement in East Jerusalem, which it considered detrimental to the peace process with the Palestinians. The Palestinians, like the administration, had made a settlement freeze the cornerstone of their policy and a condition for negotiations. The decision to allow Moskowitz from Miami to go ahead with his building project in Sheikh Jarrah, an Arab neighborhood that had become the focus of international attention against Israeli settlement in Jerusalem, was an open slap in the face to the American administration that had expressly made it known that any such move would be highly unappreciated.

The incident caused such a dip in Israel-U.S. relations, already slighted by Joe Biden's March 2010 visit coinciding with newly approved settlements, that Netanyahu was called to Washington to try to repair the damage. On March 23, barely two weeks after the Biden visit and the Ramat Shlomo fiasco, just hours before Netanyahu's scheduled meeting with Obama, almost unbelievably, the Jerusalem municipality announced formal approval for Moskowitz to build twenty Jewish housing units on the site of the Shepherd's Hotel in Sheikh Jarrah. It looked to the administration as though Moskowitz was more important than the president of the United States. Israel should be staying well away from building in Arab Jerusalem. It needs the Arab villages surrounding it like a diabetic needs sugar. Before the 1967 war, Jews made up 94 percent of Jerusalem's population. When it annexed the Old City and East Jerusalem in 1967, Israel added 44,000 Arabs to the demographic balance and then when it decided to add seventy square kilometers and several West Bank villages to its municipal border, it inherited 22,000 more Arabs, who forty years later numbered many times that and just in annual social security payments cost Israel somewhere in the region of $240 million a year.

After 1967 Jerusalem's population grew to 264,000, of whom only 74 percent were Jewish. By the end of 2010 the population had almost tripled, at 750,000, and the percentage of Jews was down to 64 percent. Despite the high birthrate of ultraorthodox

Jews, the Arabs are more prolific. In 2010, 42 percent of Arabs in Jerusalem were under age fifteen, as opposed to only 31 percent of the Jews. Given the exodus of young Israelis from the city, and even of young ultraorthodox families to settlements on the West Bank, where housing is cheaper, the numbers are not to Israel's advantage. Not only do the Arabs not leave the city, but they are attracted to stay, as Jerusalem residency affords them most of the rights of an Israeli citizen, including probably the best health care and social services in the Middle East. Work in traditional Arab trades, like construction, is plentiful in Jerusalem, and salaries are good. Though over the years only 6 percent have opted for Israeli citizenship, all Arab Jerusalem residents have a blue ID card allowing total freedom of movement throughout Israel, making them an important bridge to the West Bank. So while Jews leave, Arabs will stay and the future of Jerusalem being Israel's undivided and eternal capital will be jeopardized, unless, of course, as part of a peace agreement someone does the entirely logical thing and sheds the outlying Palestinian villages and predominantly Arab neighborhoods from Israeli Jerusalem. It should be done as quickly as possible. The millions a year Israel pays out to Palestinians in Silwan, Shuafat, Sur Baher, Umm Tuba, Beit Hanina, and other Arab villages that have almost nothing to do with Jerusalem is but the tip of the iceberg if one takes into account infrastructure, schools, clinics, and municipal services. The reason these villages are part of Jerusalem has nothing to do with the Bible, history, or geography, but rather that the head of the Central Command at the time, Rehavam Ze'evi, who later went into politics on a platform that called for the transfer of Israeli Arabs out of the country, thought they were important to protect

Jerusalem's integrity, a security belt in which only strategic factors played a part, not the real people who lived in it.

Now Arab and Jewish Jerusalem are seemingly evermore irrevocably interlocked. Each success by Elad or Ateret Cohanim is another blow for a solution ever being found that could satisfy both Israeli and Palestinian demands to have Jerusalem as their capital. Or so it would seem. In truth most of the Jewish settlements built on the Arab side, other than clear provocations by ideologically motivated groups, could be incorporated into Jewish Jerusalem in the future. There is also a very clear line in the city, albeit jigsawlike, between east and west, between Arabs and Jews. The difference is not marked by any border; there is no fence or marker and no checkpoints. The architecture of much of the buildings is the same, particularly the public buildings erected in Ottoman and British times. Streets and avenues run into one another, but you know very quickly which side of town you are on. Even on common ground like the Jerusalem Promenade of Liberty Bell Garden, you can see the delineation between Arabs and Jews, in the dress, bicycles, number of children, and what's cooking on the little tin coal barbecues people use at picnics.

I live in Abu Tor on the Israeli side of the seam between east and west. Come for a walk with me a few blocks to the east into Arab Abu Tor and on to Silwan, or just a short way to the south to Jabal Mukaber, the Mount of Evil Counsel, also the home to UN headquarters, and you won't be entering a different suburb or even a different city; it's like entering a different world. The neat, tree-lined streets with recycling bins for plastic bottles and newspapers give way to mayhem and chaos with children running across roads with no regard to the traffic, people parked where they like, and graffiti all over the walls. Loud music blares and piles of garbage are thrown next to empty trash bins. Barber shops, garages, bakers, fruit vendors, and *punkcheriot*—tire puncture fixers—seem to be everywhere. There is little order, no decorum, and little logic to things, like the pharmacy serving falafel through a side window. The signs are in Arabic, and Jewish custom, for the most part, is not welcome. I was told by the hardware store that they had no nails and did not sell hammers. Every fourth house or so has a banner and artwork attesting that one of its oc-cupants has been on the hajj, pilgrimage, to Mecca; the minarets of mosques can be seen all over and five times a day, every day, the muezzin calls the faithful to prayer. In these villages, now part of greater Jerusalem, the women wear dark, thick raincoats in summer, and no teenage girl has her head uncovered. Strollers are rarely seen, though children are everywhere, and though most of the cars are older models puffing out exhaust fumes, they are adorned with brightly colored gadgets and sound systems that compete with the multiple muezzins and their loudspeakers in volume.

Having the two distinct sides to the same city seemingly gives credence to the concept that Jerusalem is at the center of the conflict with the Palestinians, that it is one of those complex issues in the peace process that is impossible to resolve, or at least impossibly difficult to resolve. Jerusalem is complex religiously, socially, and even politically, but in terms of Arabs and Jews and the peace process, it is not beyond resolution. Both the Jews and the Palestinians claim it as their capital, a seemingly irreconcilable situation. But it is not. The 1980 Jerusalem Law says the city is

Israel's undivided capital but specifies no boundaries, while Abu Dis, just over the security barrier in the West Bank, the location of a building meant to house the Palestinian parliament, is closer to the Temple Mount than the Knesset is. Many have tabled solutions, including the Geneva Initiative and specialists like Danny Seidemann, a Jerusalem lawyer who founded the Ir Amim organization and has devoted most of his professional life to the issue of Jerusalem and peace, and Shaul Arieli, who used to be the mapmaker for the defense establishment; these two men could draw the borders between east and west in their sleep. They could show you highways that connect Ramallah, the current seat of Palestinian government, and Abu Dis, where the parliament was to be, without having to go through Israeli territory. They could point out where security checkpoints should be on the outskirts of the city to ensure the security of those inside, and to obviate the need for barriers between the sides inside the city itself.

If the sides decide to make peace, the hard work of how to divide Jerusalem has been done. Instead of Jerusalem being an impediment to peace, it should be a bridge to understanding. The exit from the newly excavated tunnel adjacent to the Western Wall comes out in the Via Dolorosa, the paths of the two religions crossing at the Fourteenth Station. Less than a hundred meters away is the Muslim Quarter where merchants sell T-shirts with "Israel I Love You" on them and bottles of holy baptismal water from the River Jordan. It is a place not of contention, but where tolerance allows people freedom and where borders are ephemeral, not physical. There is nothing like mid-afternoon on a Friday when the Muslims go home from prayer and the Jews prepare for the Sabbath, a quiet that is a spiritual interlude between those who share this city, or those periods of the year when the three religions celebrate their festivals, each to their own God, each in their own way, and all in Jerusalem. In spring it is Passover and Easter and in winter Hanukkah and Christmas and sometimes the Muslim feasts of Eid al-Adha and Eid al-Fitr, the Muslim calendar not having a leap year in it, giving them an extra day every four years and putting them out of sync with the rest of us.

While few challenge Muslim religious claims to the city and accept that Muslims consider Al Aksa the third-holiest site of Islam, there are those who argue that the Palestinians never had a political capital in Jerusalem and that the demand is ludicrous, which may be true. But it is also true that the Palestinians have never had a state before, Israel has never had to make peace with them before, and the Arab villages of Jerusalem have never been considered part of Jerusalem before. We live with new realities and have been posed with the challenge of resolving them. Jerusalem is not the problem, but part of the solution. There is great justice to the city being honorably shared by Israel and the Palestinians in the hope for a better common future. Neither of the parties should see the city as "theirs," but rather as holding it in trusteeship for the rest of the world, ensuring that the freedom of religion and respect for the holy places that now exist remains in place for generations to come. In that role of shared responsibility, together with international support, the moving of embassies to Jerusalem, and hopefully the headquarters of international organizations as well, the city could be the magnet for peace and stability, and not the game spoiler of the peace process. If, however, the complications of Jerusalem are allowed to fester, with the vacuum being filled by Elad and Ateret Cohanim, or Palestinian provocateurs who throw stones at every opportunity, Jerusalem will revert to being a backwater and a problem.

There is a stone deep under the Dome of the Rock on which it is traditionally believed that Abraham prepared to sacrifice Isaac and from where Mohammed is said to have ascended to heaven. That is a rock of shared belief. So Jerusalem is destined to become a city of shared sovereignty and mutual coexistence, regardless of whether it is this generation of peacemakers who achieve it. In Jerusalem Israel has its Knesset, seat of government, Supreme Court, Yad Vashem, and national institutions. Israel's capital does not need Jabal Mukaber or Sheikh Jarrah. It can only benefit Jerusalem to have the Palestinians consider it their capital and hopefully invest in its development and beautification. How wonderful it would be to see the Arab part of the city shining as well, and for Jerusalem to become as tranquil every day of the week as it is on a normal Friday afternoon.

 THIRTEEN

Israel Internal:
A Narrow Bridge to Cross

I have often been accused of being an optimist about Israel, a serious charge in a country that considers paranoia a virtue. I can certainly appreciate those who see black on the horizon: so many of the problems Israel faces seem out of proportion to the size of a small country. It is as if the country lives on edge all the time, constantly dealing with emergencies, lacking time to pause and take stock. Even when things are on an even keel something, somehow, will create a crisis to buffet the entire nation. Where are the days of Ben Gurion, Begin, Rabin—people you may not have agreed with politically but had infinite trust in, knowing that the nation was their primary concern, not their own political survival? All three did what they thought was the right thing for Israel, despite massive internal opposition: Ben Gurion accepted a state without Jewish Jerusalem, Begin defied his own maximalist ideologies and made peace with Egypt, and Rabin shook Arafat's hand and sealed the Oslo Accords. Each paid a heavy price for their leadership. Ben Gurion receded into retirement in the desert at Kibbutz Sde Boker, almost like an old Eskimo going off into the snow. Begin could not take the casualties caused by what he saw as his own weakness in not containing the first Lebanese war and gave up the will to live, dying a slow and lonely death. Rabin knew his life was on the line for making peace with the Palestinians, defied the threats, attended a peace rally, and sang the song of peace, his gruff, cigarette-laden voice husky over the microphone, and then he was shot. Ben Gurion lived in a hut in the Negev, Begin in a modest rented apartment in Jerusalem, and Rabin in a regular apartment block in Ramat Aviv that was comfortable but nothing out of the ordinary. The legendary finance minister Pinhas Sapir, who is credited with building modern Israel, lived in a tiny shack in Kfar Saba. When I was a young Knesset reporter, I used to give Israel Kargman, the chairman of the powerful Finance Committee, a lift to the central bus station on my way back to the newsroom.

The current generation, the second generation, the fifty- to sixty-year-olds in the Knesset and at the head of public service around 2011, are different. They are opportunists, moving from one political party to the next, fiddling with ideologies as if they were tools in a survival game, not beacons of light along the way. The second generation has been unable to differentiate between duty, fealty, and self-enrichment, thinking they were entitled because they ascended to power. A former Israeli president, Moshe Katsav, was convicted in 2010 on two counts of rape, which he committed while serving as a minister in the Israeli government.

A prime minister, Ehud Olmert, was indicted in August 2009 on three charges of corruption. In the same year a former health minister, Shlomo Benizri, was sentenced to four years for theft, fraud, and obstructing justice. In July 2008 Olmert's finance minister, Avraham Hirschson, was sentenced to five years and five months for breach of trust, aggravated fraud, theft, forgery, and money laundering. In 2007 the justice minister, Haim Ramon, was convicted of indecent assault and sent to do community service, his political career in near ruin. This generation has shown little modesty: Ehud Barak lived in a multimillion-dollar apartment in the swishy Akirov Building in Tel Aviv while head of the nationally socialist Labor Party; Ariel Sharon, while still a general, managed to wrangle himself a huge estate, the Sycamore Ranch, in which the Ewing brothers, the oil barons from the *Dallas* soap opera, would be proud to live; Binyamin Netanyahu, in addition to an apartment in Rehavia in Jerusalem, owned an impressive house in exclusive Caesarea, and the list goes on.

Despite the change in norms, there are those who say that Israel is still a shtetl, a small Jewish village somewhere in Eastern Europe, where everyone knows everyone else's business. This is particularly true with the country's rich, where twenty-three business groups, often family businesses, control 40 percent of the market. You read the economic section of the morning paper and you think you are on a merry-go-round: Dankner sells to Arison; Arison sells to Tshuva; Tshuva buys from Levayev, who sells to Dankner, who bought from Ofer and sold to Arison, all of whom bought a piece of Arison to finance Dankner's new venture with Ofer.

Some of this is new wealth, much of it because in 1948, when Israel desperately needed refining capacity and other basic infrastructure, there were very few families who could finance the new industries. The Ofers, for example, who had made a fortune in shipping in the aftermath of the Second World War, had the money and gained control of the refining industry and much of Israel's chemical wealth for generations to come. They also controlled the shipping industries. Others came along, in particular the Arisons, who made their fortune in the U.S. shipping industry, returned to Israel, and bought Israel's largest bank. Some of the money is from luck. Yekutiel Federmann, an immigrant of modest means, owned the patisserie Yardenia on the Carmel in Haifa during the British mandate. One day a British officer left a briefcase behind, which Federmann found and opened to see whether he could learn the identity of the person who had lost it. Inside he came across top-secret British plans for the relocation of their main supply base from Alexandria, which had become more vulnerable to German attack, to Haifa. There was also a list of the supplies the British urgently needed, which Federmann rushed to fulfill. By the time the flustered British officer came back for his briefcase, Federmann was pleased to hand it over, together with a promise for 20,000 pairs of military khaki shorts by the next morning. Though a baker, Federmann contacted a friend who knew a friend at the Ata textile factory near Haifa who understood the potential involved. By the next morning, the British officer had his order and Federmann was appointed as one of the main suppliers to the British and Allied forces during the war or, as some put it, received a license to print money in hard times. Federmann built the Dan Hotel chain in the 1950s, later including the Jerusalem King David Hotel among his portfolio. Under the tutelage of Yekutiel's son Michael, the family was cited as

Israel's thirteenth wealthiest in 2009, owning vast tracts of real estate and, among other things, Elbit, a major electronics and defense company. Yitzhak Tshuva became an oil baron from nothing, and a massive property owner in New York, including the Plaza Hotel; the Proper and Straus families made their fortunes in food connecting up with Nestle and other international conglomerates. Alfred Akirov, a diminutive man whose father was an immigrant from Iraq, is one of the country's biggest builders. There are many others but the country's wealth remains concentrated in the hands of a few, several hundred families, now with a sprinkling of new high-tech millionaires and former generals who have made it rich with outside security contracts, and the respectable element of the oligarchs who flooded Israel after the collapse of the former Soviet Union. They open museums together and attend one another's social events. They give to one another's charities, serve on one another's boards, and have undue influence over the country's political system, particularly since the introduction of a primary system in the main parties, an automatic magnet for the potent mix of money and power.

The good news in all of this is that although Israel is young, it has the institutions that can root out evil. It sends presidents, prime ministers, justice ministers, and finance ministers to jail when they break the law, and the justice system remains impervious to any outside influences. The state comptroller, the attorney general, and the Supreme Court are the arbiters of right and wrong and have thus far proved impeccable. The police have had a few rotten apples, but in Israel the law remains paramount. The press is almost vengeful in its attack on public impropriety, to the point that politicians actually have to worry about their pasts when running for office. A flirt gone wrong after one too many drinks on a night out at a conference cost a candidate for police chief his job in 2010, and a war hero with many years of distinguished service to his credit, Yoav Gallant, was rejected in 2011 for the post of chief of staff after it was found that he had lied to a court over a land appropriation issue five years before.

In many senses Israel is indeed a town, given its small size and population density. Local issues become national ones with ease, and the plenum of the Knesset more often resembles the floor of a parochial marketplace than the country's main legislative body. When a soldier is lost, the loss is felt by all, and when gas is discovered off Israel's shores, the feeling is that one's uncle has just won the lottery. Because of universal military service, other than exemptions for most ultraorthodox and the Arab minority, there is a feeling of shared burden, and when a soldier is kidnapped and taken captive, his return becomes an issue for the entire country. On June 26, 2006, Gilad Shalit, a corporal in the IDF armor corps, was kidnapped in a cross-border raid from Gaza by Hamas. Since then he has been held in a secret location, all visits to him forbidden, while Hamas has demanded the release of 1,000 Palestinian prisoners, many of them convicted terrorists, in exchange for Shalit. Despite the intensive efforts of a German mediator, almost five years later Shalit had still not been released, the prime minister deeming the price too high, though other prime ministers have made disproportionate deals for the release of Israelis in the past. Some of the terrorists being demanded for Shalit by Hamas have rivers of blood on their hands and have been sentenced to multiple life terms. (Israel has a death penalty on its statute books, but except in the single case of Adolf Eichmann has never enforced it.)

Some of the families of those killed by the terrorists and others, primarily from the Israeli right wing, have opposed their release. But almost five years after his capture, Shalit's family and friends were still holding a vigil in a white tent outside the prime minister's residence in Jerusalem and despite the passage of time hundreds, if not thousands, of people from all over the country continued to visit the tent in homage to the strength of the family and to offer their support. Songs have been written about Shalit and entire busloads of schoolchildren stop by almost daily, the children wearing blue and white "Free Gilad Shalit" T-shirts and holding yellow ribbons. On Friday nights members of a local synagogue move their Sabbath services to the Shalit tent and volunteers bring over a Sabbath meal to share with the family. Almost every car that passes flicks its lights or honks softly in support of the family and in recognition of their vigil, telling the Shalits that they are not alone. And they are not alone. What happened to Gilad could happen to any of our children, and the flick of the lights or short honk says "we are with you," just as we know they would be there for us. That's why this shtetl works.

Not so when it comes to politics. Several hundred feet away from the Shalit tent, surrounded by a high stone wall with electronic sensors and alarms on top, and guards with earpieces and semiautomatic rifles, is the official residence of the prime minister of Israel, who was Ehud Olmert when Shalit was captured. Olmert's diplomatic efforts to secure Shalit's release failed. Binyamin Netanyahu, who inherited the Shalit drama, could have finished the deal in December 2009 but got cold feet at the last minute. A list of around 460 prisoners to be released had been drawn up and vetted by the security services, with some of the most dangerous terrorists being slated for exile, and others to be released into Gaza. With all the paperwork done and the deal imminent, Netanyahu backtracked, to the fury of the German and Israeli negotiators, one of whom, an Israeli, later told me in disgust that I had a "prime minister with no balls."

By all accounts, Netanyahu had all the credentials to be a highly skilled prime minister, not one who would have gotten cold feet over a deal with Hamas that would have enjoyed wide public support, or one to preside over a fiasco like the East Jerusalem building incident at such a sensitive period in relations between Israel and the United States. At the time, Netanyahu was serving his second term as prime minister, having been hauled over the coals the first time between 1996 and 1999 by his coalition partners and later the electorate. In the interim he served as a highly successful finance minister in Ariel Sharon's government and between his mistakes the first time around and tutelage under Sharon, it was assumed he had learned something. Netanyahu also is no fool. He has a double degree from Ivy League American universities, in architecture and mathematics. He served time as a diplomat in the foreign ministry and as Israel's ambassador to the UN, was an officer in one of the country's most elite military units, and came from a highly respectable family. On paper Netanyahu had all the credentials to lead and to succeed. But somehow the curriculum vitae and reality did not add up. He gives the impression of being a juggler, always having balls in the air, more dedicated to holding his coalition together than to the future of the country.

The same rule could be applied to those around Netanyahu's cabinet table: person by person, these were probably the most competent ministers ever to lead Israel, professors and doctors, lawyers and accountants, former chiefs of staff and heads of the secret service. Generally they were relatively young, erudite, well-educated, and well-traveled, and had done military service. They were mostly sabras, born in Israel; those born outside Israel had arrived young. Politically, however, they were a long leap from collectively forming a competent government. On the contrary, those around the cabinet table were riven by rivalries and intrigue, and motivated by the narrow interests of their parties rather than the national good. They did not agree on issues of state and religion, the peace process, or social issues, but had been cobbled together to form a majority of votes in the Knesset so that Netanyahu could form a government without his main rival, Tzipi Livni of the Kadima Party.

The Netanyahu government in 2011 was indicative of Israel's curse: a democratic electoral system that makes it almost impossible to govern, other than in exceptional cases, when leaders like Ben Gurion, Begin, Rabin, and Sharon were able to move mountains despite the system. It's a system that leads to a tyranny of the minority. Small parties representing narrow interests become the decisive power brokers. Only once in Israel's history has a cluster of like-minded parties enjoyed a majority of seats in the Knesset, in 1968 when the Alignment for the first and only time in Israel's history had the barest pure majority, 61 out of 120 seats in the Knesset, enough seats to rule.

Almost anyone and their mother can form a political party, and it takes only 2 percent of the electorate to place someone in the Knesset. In 2009, thirty-three parties contested the elections, including the Green Leaf Party, the Green-Meimad Party, the Green Party, the Holocaust Survivor–Green Leaf Alumni Party, the Man's Rights in the Family Party, Power to the Family Party, the Bread Party, the Power of Money Party, and any of two dozen others standing for election. Each of these crackpot political enterprises gets free radio and television time. The man from the Man's Rights party cowered on television and complained of being beaten by his wife—his claim for eligibility for a Knesset seat to represent the many out there like him.

All of this would be funny if the result was not so catastrophic. Few governments carry out their four-year terms. The Netanyahu government sworn in on April 1, 2009, was Israel's thirty-second government in sixty-one years, a record comparable only to Italy's, perhaps. In consequence, national policies and strategic planning are compromised in the most basic sense, there is little continuity in government offices where top bureaucrats change with ministers, and in the end it is democracy that is mocked.

Israelis are well aware of this and there have been attempts at electoral reform that have failed, like the change to the law that allowed for the direct election of the prime minister, legislated in 1992 and abandoned in 2001 because it caused even more fragmentation of the political system. Any attempt to move away from the current system to one that would limit the number of parties, provide for regional representation, or raise the floor of 2 percent for entry into the Knesset have all been blocked by the small parties who survive because they tilt the balance of power, a role they are not prepared to give up.

The electoral curse Netanyahu faced is typical of Israeli governments over the years. To form a government he brought in Yisrael Beiteinu, a party composed mainly of immigrants from the former Soviet Union, which emerged from the elections with fifteen mandates and a platform that challenged not only the religious status quo in Israel but also the very foundations of its democracy, demanding among other things a parliamentary commission of inquiry into the funding of NGOs that "undermine the state and support terrorism," meaning the Israeli Left, and an obligatory oath of allegiance to the Jewish state for new immigrants who are not eligible under the Law of Return, meaning Arabs. Avigdor Lieberman, who assumed the role of foreign minister in Netanyahu's government and whose ministry is credited with almost destroying Israel's relations with Turkey, was vociferously opposed to the building freeze in the territories the Obama administration wanted, or to any concessions that would limit Israel's right to build in East Jerusalem. He also made known that he would never support any peace bid by Netanyahu and that he considered the Palestinians people Israel could never live with in peace. Another coalition partner was Shas, the ultraorthodox Sephardic party that opposed Lieberman on everything to do with state and religion, opposed Netanyahu on the peace process, opposed the government's social policies, opposed the government's attempts at broadening general education, and was behind some of the most regressive and repressive anti-Arab initiatives in Israel's history, such as not allowing Jews to rent out rooms and houses to Arabs. A third partner was the secular Labor Party, fragmented from within and a shadow of its former self under the precarious leadership of Ehud Barak, who supported Netanyahu on peace but was at odds with Yisrael Beiteinu over civil rights, and with Shas on religious issues. Barak then split from Labor midterm, leading to the resignation of some ministers, who were replaced by new ones, leading to yet another dislocation in the government offices in which they had served. A fourth partner in the coalition was the Jewish Home Party, a right-wing nationalist coalition dead opposed to any concessions to the Palestinians or any thought of territorial compromise, and in deep agreement with Lieberman that Israel should somehow expel its Arabs if at all possible. The final coalition player was the United Torah Judaism Party, which does not fully recognize the state of Israel and its secular government but was willing to appoint a deputy minister with ministerial responsibilities, who would serve in the heathen government while holding its nose and running all the way to the bank with ridiculous subsidies for yeshiva students and their families way beyond what other citizens get in Israel, totally skewering the budget process and national priorities.

That Israel survives at all under these political circumstances is nothing short of a miracle. Critical to the future will be the emergence of a stable political system that allows for rational government. Perhaps this will happen, because old political frameworks are collapsing. The Labor Party has long been ideologically dead—the kibbutzim are the country's biggest industrialists and agriculture depends on Thai workers. The Likud has given back part of Hebron to the Palestinians, and even in Shas there is a slow but certain move away from conventional state-supported ultraorthodoxy to a more productive constituency. New centers of power are starting to emerge, like the Kadima Party, originally founded as a breakaway by Ariel Sharon prior to the 2006 elections and which has become a classic social-democratic party that seems to represent a broad base of Israeli polity. In the 2009 elections Kadima won most seats in the Knesset but its leader, Tzipi

Livni, preferred to stay in opposition rather than form a coalition she knew was doomed to fail.

By 2010 Livni's Kadima, Netanyahu's Likud, and Barak's Labor had no deep ideological differences between them. Together they controlled fifty-eight seats in the Eighteenth Knesset, a very healthy figure that if mobilized effectively could have made a huge difference to Israel's future. Together these parties could have been the pillars of a strong Jewish democratic state that cut its course toward peace and conciliation, steered away from regressive and quasi-fascist legislation, like that being put forward by Yisrael Beiteinu, and was liberated from the subsidies the religious parties demanded for their continued participation in the government. Together with some help from others in the Knesset, they could have changed the electoral system to be more representative and reflective of democracy, and rationalized state and religious issues. Had Netanyahu risen to the challenge of trying to work with Kadima instead of fighting it—seeing it as an ally in the fight against democratic tyranny rather than a political rival—Israel could be heading progressively forward. By choosing the coalition partners he did and giving in to their demands, however, Netanyahu perpetuated the governmental anarchy that eventually could be Israel's democratic downfall, as minorities muscle their beliefs onto the national stage at national expense. How Israel will look in the future is as unpredictable as the flip of a coin. If the majority organize and lead, the country will remain democratic. If quasi-fascist legislation, the type Lieberman and his party want to become the norm, continues, the country will look and be different indeed. If Shas continues to put through edicts that look as if they came out of the Middle Ages, even though the party has less than 10 percent representation in the House, Israeli democracy will gently morph into a de facto theocracy.

For Israel to survive as a democratic Jewish state, the status quo has to change. It has become a national imperative. With the founding fathers off center stage and old ideologies eroded, there is a chance for a serious social-democratic party to lead toward this change, but the leader of this silent majority has yet to emerge. Still, a new generation in the Knesset has yet to make its voice heard. That's where the optimists are looking.

Other than its political system, there are two other critical internal factors that will decide what type of country Israel will be: the ultraorthodox and Israeli Arabs, two communities that are growing fast and are not exactly Zionist in their outlook. If things continue along their present course, according to the Taub Center for Social Policy Studies in Jerusalem, an independent think tank, by 2040 some 78 percent of Israelis in primary school will be either ultraorthodox or Arab, with tremendous consequences for Israel, not only as a democracy but also in terms of its very existence. The ultraorthodox have a birthrate of 6.5 percent per year, doubling in size every 11.5 years, while 56 percent of them technically live below the poverty line, as opposed to only 15 percent of the rest of the population. The enrollment of ultraorthodox children in primary schools has risen 50 percent in ten years. In 1948, when Ben Gurion as first prime minister gave full-time yeshiva students state financing and exemption from army service, the number of students involved was four hundred. In 2010 it had grown to more than 60,000, a massive cumulative increase that will accelerate as the numbers grow. In all, 60 percent of Orthodox men do not work, as opposed to less than 15 percent of the rest of the population, and only 50 percent of ultraorthodox women work, as opposed to 80 percent of other Jewish women in Israel.

Worse, in addition to the general ire toward the Hareidim, as the ultraorthodox call themselves, literally meaning "in fear," they have been found to bite the hand that feeds them, operating massive scams that empty the national treasury. For several years now the country's largest selling paper, *Yedioth Ahronoth*, has been investigating the ultraorthodox community. In December 2010 they decided to test enrollment figures at four yeshivot, institutions of Torah study, which receive state funds according to the number of students enrolled. The Minchat Yitzhak Kolel received state subsidies for 698 students on its books; only 59 students were actually enrolled. The rest were fictitious. Eidat Yerushalayim received money for 136 students; there were actually 14. And Oztar Hachochmah—the treasury of wisdom—was very wise, receiving stipends for 165 students, when the school did not in fact exist at all. Periodic Hareidi outbursts also add to the general public's anger toward them. They stopped the building of an underground emergency ward at a hospital in Ashkelon, close to the Gaza Strip and therefore vulnerable to rocket attack, because of some ancient graves that might or might not have been Jewish. They were later proved not to be. Millions of dollars were wasted in lost time, excavations, and added costs for what turned out to be nothing more than a Hareidi attempt by one of the factions to move the emergency room to nearby Ashdod, where they operate and own a hospital that could have used the investment. Amos Biderman drew a cartoon in *Ha'aretz* the morning after all this was discovered, showing Hareidim dancing in a graveyard, their hair locks twirling in the wind, showering hundreds of dollars onto skeletons; his caption read "The Grateful Dead." There have been riots over parking issues on the Sabbath in Jerusalem, and the courts have found overt racism in some Hareidi schools where Sephardic children were banned from studying with their Ashkenazi peers. And then there was a national uproar over some bus services that had given in to the demand of the Hareidim to have women sit at the back of the bus, introducing gender-segregated bus lines in some areas. On top of it all was that the overwhelming majority of Hareidi men avoided any form of national service whatsoever. Combined with the yeshiva scam and the disproportionate welfare benefits, this made them parasites in the eyes of many Israelis. By 2010 the ultraorthodox issue had become a major item on Israel's national agenda, with many predicting a black future—literally, since the ultraorthodox wear predominantly black—unless major changes were made. In December 2009 Israel's population was 7.5 million, of which 5.66 million were Jewish. At that time the Hareidi population was placed at 736,000, growing at more than twice the rate of the rest of Israel's Jews. The good news, however, was that some of the ultraorthodox leaders have begun to recognize that the gravy train would soon be leaving the station unless they themselves began to encourage change. Slowly, slowly the shackles that kept the Hareidim behind the wall of the ghetto were starting to be removed. Women have been encouraged to work, particularly in telephone service jobs they can do from home; others have entered human care services and secretarial jobs that are appropriate in terms of modesty. A dent has been made with subsidies: to receive them religious schools must teach core subjects like arithmetic, English, geography, sciences, and civil society. Some rabbis have given the nod to establishing special colleges that teach such professions as accountancy, programming, auxiliary medical services, and community services. Courses have been set up that have drawn Hareidi men into the prison service, police, and Magen David Adom, the Israeli Red Cross.

Even enrollment into the army increased, with special battalions established that catered to the special needs of ultraorthodox soldiers, such as strictly kosher food and an appropriate distance from women. In 2007 enrollment into Hareidi battalions was 340 men; in 2009 it had grown to 1,180 and in 2011 to 2,400, with a goal of 4,800 by 2015. It is a beginning. Outside Israel the number of ultraorthodox men who are perpetual students is very small. Almost the entire community works and some are extremely prosperous and generous. The term "poverty" when applied to the Hareidi community is very different than when applied, for example, to south-side Chicago. There is no hunger, no illiteracy, and virtually no violent crime on the streets. There are soup kitchens, free medical equipment, schools that go from early morning till late in the afternoon with hot meals, and community support and massive philanthropy from diamond merchants and other Hareidim who have become mega-wealthy. If one goes to Mea Sha'arim, the closed ultraorthodox quarter of Jerusalem, one quickly understands that while the statistics may say otherwise, there is a vibrant underground economy with money changing hands and disappearing into tills that would not know a receipt if they saw one.

"Ultraorthodox" is also a very broad, loosely used term with significant differences between the various sects. Some are Zionist, others passive about Zionism and open to receiving the benefits offered by the modern Jewish state, while still others are so opposed to the modern Zionist state that they became best friends with Yasser Arafat in his time and with Iran's leaders, who are openly dedicated to Israel's destruction. Some burn the Israeli flag on Independence Day and refuse to stand in silence when the two-minute siren wails to commemorate Israel's war dead, while others are starting to perform military and national service. In this mix are the Belz, Bobov, Bosterners, Breslav, Chabad, Lubavich, Ger, Karlin, Munkacz, Puppa, and Vizhnitz Hassidic sects, which have varying degrees of a symbiotic relationship with Israel, and then the anti-Zionists, like the Satmar, Dushinsky, Toldos Aharon, Naturei Karta, Toldos Avraham Yitzhak, and the Litvishers, to mention but a few. Shas, the Sephardic ultraorthodox movement, is Zionist and active in government, while the Agudat Yisrael and the United Torah Judaism Party play from the sidelines. Each has a different attitude toward work and study: some are inward, while others conduct outreach. Each wears a different uniform, some with furry hats, others with white socks tucked into their pants, some with black Pandora hats with a tip in the front, others with round hats like the one worn by Tuvia the milkman in the classic *Fiddler on the Roof* musical. Each of these sects has its own supreme rabbi and, therefore, its own rigid religious principles. To see them as one bloc is a mistake. They share a common belief in stringent religious practice, but in all other matters the margins are wide.

The discipline the Hareidim have toward a supreme leader, the rebbe, makes change easier as everyone automatically follows his rulings; if you can convince one person that change is necessary, it will be carried through the ranks with near-total discipline. Until around 2000 the Hareidim would not live in multistory buildings, not wanting to take an elevator on the Sabbath even though automatic elevators have been used by Orthodox Jews for many years. Then, when the state offered extremely cheap housing in tall buildings being built in new ultraorthodox towns with good schools, excellent community services, like-minded neighbors, and an excellent quality of Hareidi life, the rabbis decided that the Shabbat elevators were kosher and their followers moved there in droves.

Another side of the Hareidi community is typified by Shas, a party whose strength is found among traditional Sephardic Jews from the lower socioeconomic levels of Israeli society. The movement's spiritual leader was Rabbi Ovadia Yosef, whose word was law, and who together with his disciples managed to navigate Shas admirably through Israeli politics. Unfortunately, the religious school system Shas created with government funding failed to prepare their children for the real world. It concentrated only on religious education, thereby perpetuating the cycle of poverty and state dependence. There were, however, key people in Shas who wanted to break this. In December 2010 Rabbi Chaim Amsellem, a Shas member of the Knesset, stunned everyone when he broke party ranks and called on the cycle of poverty to be broken, for the Hareidim to move into the workplace and to get an education that would serve them in the future while continuing to serve God's commandments meticulously. There was no contradiction between the two, he said. On the contrary, work and earning one's bread honorably was a divine decree. Those yeshiva students who were brilliant should be supported as future scholars, judges, and rabbis, and should be allowed to study forever, he said. The rest should get out and work, as is proper in any society. The Shas newspaper called him "Amalek," Israel's most heinous biblical enemy, and called for him to be wiped out, as the Israelites did to the miserable tribe at the time, but his words resonated deeply and put the subject squarely on the table in a way his colleagues and country could not ignore. The issue has been simmering for years. The 4,000 ultraorthodox who will come out of the army will do so as skilled workers—mechanics, computer technicians, clerks, electricians. They will also come out with a broader worldview and friendships beyond the narrow confines of the ghetto. They may form 4,000 families less dependent upon welfare, gainfully employed, more integrated into Israeli society, and more deeply identified with Israel's national goals. It is a beginning. Statistics are statistics and social scientists are right to sound alarms, but that should not close people's eyes to the changes that are already taking place, to the crack that has appeared. Zionism came out of the ghetto, and those who founded this country came from homes not different from those in the ultraorthodox neighborhoods of Geula or Mea Shearim today.

The ultraorthodox mainstream is, for the most part, an ultimately pragmatic community. They will find a way to adapt, as they always have. At some point they will stop being a burden on Israeli society and, in their own way, will live here as they do in Golders Green, Borough Park, Brookline, or Antwerp. The geniuses will be kept studying and teaching and the rest will work to support their families and their communities. To do this they will have to interact with the rest of Israeli society and if, as Israeli citizens, they are found eligible for national service in one form or another, they will do it. The same exemptions that apply to other students in Israel will apply to them, with sensitivity to their special needs. They will continue to live in their own worlds but will become more a part of Israel's universe. On the fringes of Hareidi society are groups that will never change and never adapt, but their numbers are small and their influence minimal. For the rest, as Israel gets older and they become more and more Israeli, they will become more part of Israel. The Hareidi community is by far the youngest community in Israel. They also tend to have children at a relatively early age. Most are second- or third-generation Israelis. Their leadership is increasingly Israel-born. The snow-swept plains of Galicia and the reason for their furry hats is an increasingly distant memory, and more and more they are encountering the anger and impatience of the rest of Israel, which is tired of being taken to the cleaners and then having to shine their shoes as well. If the Hareidim don't adjust, there will inevitably be a major backlash against them. The status quo is untenable and I believe no one knows that better than the Hareidi leadership themselves. Traditionally the ultraorthodox have been the holders of the balance in Israeli coalitions, but there could be a coalition without them if the country's public reaches a point where they feel the problem threatens national survival. A precedent came with the first Sharon government in 2001, when the Hareidim were excluded from the coalition, subsidies to them were cut drastically, and funds for their educational system were made conditional on their including core subjects in their curriculum. The key to resolving the problem is the legislation and implementation of universal national service for all Israeli citizens, be it in the military or the security services, hospitals, nursing homes, work with the disadvantaged, agriculture, and even service abroad with either Jewish communities in distress or aid to the Third World in a Peace Corps–type program.

Universal service is the way to integrate, not only the Harei-dim, but also the Israeli Arabs into Israeli society. Implementing it is critical to Israel's remaining a forward-looking democracy with equality for all its citizens, both in terms of benefits and commitments. Without universal national service, the Hareidim and Israeli Arabs will remain on the periphery of Israeli society, will increasingly become resented by the rest of the country, and will suffer from bigotry and discrimination as a result. Universal national service could stop that cycle. If Jews perform national service in Arab sectors and Arabs perform theirs in Jewish communities, understanding between the sides will deepen, old wounds will heal, and a foundation for new understandings will be laid. Most important, two time bombs that are clearly on Israel's doorstep will be defused, if not fully resolved, for the betterment of all.

For Israeli Arabs, national service in itself is not a panacea for the complicated problems they face as a minority community in a country that is at endless war with people they consider brethren. Serving a country they feel is not theirs and, worse, an impostor on their land at their expense is complicated, but Israeli Arab politicians who serve in the Knesset face the same dilemma in terms of the degree with which they take part in Israeli society. No Arab has ever been more than a token member of any Israeli government, and no serious Arab politician would consider such a position. But the Knesset is something else, the floor of democracy, the place where all groups and all interests in the country

try to establish their agendas, make their voices heard, even if they are keen opponents of the Zionist state.

Similarly, no one is expecting masses of Israeli Arabs to rush to join the Israeli army, but if their national service is in hospitals, which serve the Israeli Arab community extensively, schools, services, and other aspects of society that serve the Arabs as well, they will be benefiting their own, not only the Jewish state. They will gain knowledge and experience they can bring back with them to their communities. With national service they can integrate into Israeli society without giving up their identity, and continue to live their lives as probably the most advantaged Arab community in the Middle East without threat or fear.

Israeli Arabs now compose about 20 percent of Israel's population. They are anything but homogeneous and politically very much resemble the Jews with four political parties for eleven members of Knesset. Urban Israeli Arabs and those who live in the Galilee villages are very different, and the Bedouin are a case apart again, especially in the Negev, where the community is growing very fast, experiencing growing urbanization and becoming increasingly Islamic fundamentalist in its outlook.

There are very encouraging trends in the Israeli Arab community, such as the advancement of women, growing higher educational levels, more integration into fields like the sciences and medicine, and declining birthrates. But at the same time, with more education comes a deeper questioning of identity and belonging, and a growing resentment over the economic and social discrimination that exists.

Israeli Arabs have had to bite their tongues during two intifadas that involved their own brothers fighting Israel, literally in their own backyards, and again during Israel's campaign in Gaza in 2008–2009, which left the Palestinians there decimated. Many Israeli Arabs had family members living in Gaza. They have also had to live with the guilt that while they led a life of freedom and prosperity and benefited from Israeli democracy, down the road over a million Palestinians lived under Israeli occupation, subject to searches and roadblocks and denied freedom of access and movement.

They also have to live with the knowledge that Israeli public opinion polls showed that Jewish Israelis would prefer them to be part of Palestine. In 2009, 69 percent of those polled by the Institute for National Security Studies supported the transfer of Israeli Arabs as possible to Palestine as part of a peace deal.

Even ultra-nationalists like Avigdor Lieberman, the foreign minister in Netanyahu's second government who lives on a West Bank settlement, wanted to keep much of the West Bank, and constantly spoke about Israel's need for territory to secure itself, wanted to give up Wadi Ara in the center of Israel with its 350,000 Israeli Arabs, to the Palestinians. While on most issues Lieberman was considered almost politically eccentric, on this most Israelis agreed with him.

Being a young, educated Israeli Arab must be a wrenching experience. Yet one does not sense that feeling in the university cafeteria or in the cities where young women wear traditional head coverings casually and comfortably. Young Arab students seem to be totally comfortable sitting in groups, speaking Arabic, or interacting with their Jewish counterparts. Even during the intifada it seemed that the campuses, which could have been the most explosive of environments, were calm. From time to time there have been flashpoints, particularly on the campus in Haifa, where there is a big Arab student body, and at the Hebrew University in Jerusalem, but nothing ever on the scale of the protests over student demands for lower school fees in London in 2010, for example, not even on the darkest days of the conflict. Quiescence, though, would be the wrong way to describe it. This generation of Israeli Arabs is not quiescent. Neither are they rebellious. They seem to enjoy living in Israel, with the vast majority saying that they would not want to move. Arab Christians, though a tiny minority, have greater freedom here than they do anywhere else in the Arab world. Arabs have more liberal and forward-thinking publications available to them in Israel than anywhere else in the Arab world. Despite decades of discrimination in the allocation of state funds to the Arab sector, they are partners in Israel's prosperity and enjoy one of the best health systems in the world. Ironically, or maybe indicatively, Israeli Arabs are the main contractors building the security barrier and have done extremely well in construction in general, benefiting from state infrastructure projects, and are owners of much of the trucking and heavy machinery industry in Israel.

Avigdor Lieberman and 69 percent of Israelis may want the Israeli Arabs to disappear into Palestine, but it is not going to happen. If the positive trends in the community are to be accelerated, national service is the way. Israeli Arabs are Israelis to stay. Instead of being seen as an impediment to the survivability of the Jewish state, they should be seen as a bridge to Israel's acceptance by others. They can point to the remarkable fact that though since 1948 Israel has been fighting their brethren, not since the War of Independence have there been any purges

against the Arab community in Israel, no expulsions and no ethnic cleansing. Yes, some Israeli Arabs lived under military rule
until 1965; yes, there has been discrimination, inequality in the
application of the law at times, and even police brutality in cases,
but given the objective circumstances it could have been a lot
worse. Fate has been both fortunate and cruel to the Israeli Arabs,
placing them in a country they can't identify with, but one in
which they enjoy living.

They are one-fifth of the country, growing and changing. In
some places, like the Negev, the change is fast and negative.
The Bedouin are caught in a deep social crisis that extends to
drug abuse, crime, and extended-family honor killings and a
tortured transition from a nomadic way of life to shantytowns
that lack services and infrastructure. Some Israeli Bedouin, depending on the tribe, do serve in the Israeli army, and they are
not true Palestinian Arabs in the classic sense, being wanderers
without borders or national loyalties, but rather tribal ones. The
Bedouin, now 10 percent of the Israeli Arab population, do not
have the same identity crisis other Israeli Arabs do, or the same
national aspirations. Like the Druze they fit into the mold while
looking out for themselves. National service would be of tremendous benefit to the Israeli Bedouin community, the youngest
community on earth, that is fast forgetting how to pitch a tent
and desperately needs to be absorbed into a social framework
that will allow them to integrate into society while keeping
their unique ethnic independence.

Many leaders of the Bedouin community have become alarmed
by the slide of youngsters into crime, and they themselves are
seeking a path for change. Also Israeli authorities are becoming

increasingly intolerant of Bedouin theft from Israeli farms in the Negev, and massive sabotage of national infrastructure, like water lines, from which they illegally siphon off water, and electric cables, which they steal for the copper.

There are also simmering and explosive land issues with the Bedouin that need to be resolved. Luckily for all, these are deep in the Negev and not in the center of the country and are fixable with goodwill by all sides. Bedouin, too, would benefit from required national service. They would learn trades and skills and to read and write, and be given a sense of community commitment. They could work within the government bureaucracy, learning how to lobby for their own communities and be introduced to different values that would facilitate the process of urbanization and integration for Bedouin citizens of Israel.

If the Bedouin were to bring skills back to their own communities; if Israeli Arabs did part of their national service, for example, teaching civics in Palestinian schools; if Jews were to work in Arab communities and the ultraorthodox became a productive part of life in Israel, not only would this country's chances for long-term survival as a democratic Jewish state be immeasurably enriched, but so would the lives of all those who live in it both collectively and individually. No one is asking Hareidim to stop being Hareidi, Israeli Arabs from being Arabs, or the Bedouin from being Bedouin. The goal is to create a society in which benefits and commitments are equal for all, that is proud to be heterogeneous and tolerant, Jewish and universal.

Israel is a small country and responsive when it wants to be. In the early 1960s when certain wildflowers were in danger of extinction, a campaign in the schools got children to chastise their parents for picking them. No one picks wildflowers in Israel today. The country managed to get Israelis, undisciplined, reckless, and unruly by nature, to wear seat belts and the public, long used to limitless overdrafts, to stick to credit limits. It has reacted quickly to ecological issues and to such threats as terror and forest fires.

The problem is that Israel usually reacts quickly only after the fact. In this case there is no after the fact. There is a point of no return in which it will become impossible to gainfully integrate the Hareidim and Israeli Arabs into Israeli society, and the sacrifice for this could ultimately be modern Israel itself. Everything is anchored in rationalizing the political system so that national priorities can be legislated responsibly and there can be continuity of government and policy. Social problems, once recognized, cannot be swept under the carpet with subsidies, but must be dealt with through mechanisms such as national service and a state school system that enlightens its students, not one that keeps them in the dark.

FOURTEEN

Gone the
Phantoms of the Ghetto

There are two roads from Jerusalem to Tel Aviv. Each is a different face of Israel. You can leave Jerusalem on Route 1 down the hill to Motza, up to the Kastel, past the picturesque village of Abu Gosh, and down through the forests of Sha'ar Hagai, the Forest of the Six Million, five million pine trees planted for the adults murdered in the Holocaust and a million cypresses in memory of the children who perished. You drive past the wrecks of armored cars carefully preserved in memory of those who died trying to break the siege on Jerusalem during the War of Independence. You enter the plain of Latrun, with its mysterious Trappist monastery where they make wine and chant but never speak, and through fields that change with the seasons. There are miles of vineyards, and orange groves with a scent that hangs heavy in the air when in blossom. The highway is modern, well-paved, well-lit, and well-maintained. As one nears the greater Tel Aviv area, just past Modi'in, overpasses split off in various directions, including onto the trans-Israel toll road, Highway 6, a privately owned turnkey project. Alongside the highway runs an efficient train system that is expanding and modernizing all the time, and about twenty or so kilometers east of Tel Aviv is the new main terminal at the Ben Gurion International Airport, an impressive and functional piece of architecture that has won praise from critics and travelers alike.

Or you can leave Jerusalem by way of the Begin circular road that comes out on Route 443 and proceeds west through a corridor of high cement walls, barbed-wire fences, security cameras, and watchtowers, past a hideous gray prison at the Ofer junction and onto a checkpoint manned by armed soldiers and private security guards that could for all intents and purposes be a border crossing between two countries. Route 443, much of which runs through West Bank land, was built by Yitzhak Rabin's government on the assumption that it would run the Israel-Palestine border, be a main axis connecting the West Bank with Gaza, and, at the same time, serve as an alternate route from Tel Aviv and Modi'in to Jerusalem. That was a peacetime concept, but since then Rabin was assassinated, an intifada ripped through Israel, Hamas took over Gaza, and Route 443 became a fortress.

The two roads seem almost symbolic. Route 1 offers beauty, modernity, productivity, and advancement; the alternative is the xenophobic reality of Route 443, with its fences, watchtowers, armed guards, and checkpoints. On 443 you can physically see what the future portends if Israel remains an occupier and cannot find a way to make peace with its Palestinian neighbors: life by the bayonet, massive investments in barriers and walls, and a re-ality in the holy land that makes even the biblical hills that run alongside the road look sad and forlorn. Is Israel to choose a future that will have it living in a self-imposed ghetto of security fences, watchtowers, and armed patrols, or a life of relative tranquility, of forests and fields, productivity and modernity? The choice, ul-timately, is ours to make.

Israel is not totally the master of its own destiny. It cannot make peace by itself. It cannot alone influence, let alone control, what happens in the region. When President Hosni Mubarak's Egypt fell around him in early February 2011, the best Israel could do was keep silent, say nothing, and fervently hope that the peace treaty between the countries would not unravel. There is nothing Israel can do if the masses decide to oust King Abdullah of Jordan, a sturdy leader but the head of a minority tribe in a country of rapid demographic change with a majority of Palestinians and over a million refugees from Iraq. Who knows what would be the effect on the peace treaty between the countries? Unlike Egypt, where there is a desert and a water barrier, the Suez Canal, be-tween Egyptian forces and Israel, Israel and Jordan are contiguous and close. The Egyptians have no territorial claims against Israel regardless of who leads the country. In Jordan, the Palestinians do. The Sinai is a buffer between Israel and Egypt. The West Bank is a bridge between Israel and any invader from the east. No more can Israel decide which regime will rule Syria or control the future of Lebanon, but it has to decide its future with the Palestinians. Doing so is very much key to Israel's survival, if not *the* key. Israel has to end its conquest of another people either through agreement or unilaterally. If unilateralism is the only answer, then it has to be done in a reversible way so that when peace does come, the fences can be taken down and normal relations established. In retrospect the 1993 Oslo Accords were probably premature. Yasser Arafat was a revolutionary and nationalist dedicated to liberating Palestine and saw his move to Gaza as the first concrete step along the way. The agreements also focused too much on the personalities of the individuals who made them: Arafat and Yitzhak Rabin. On the Israeli side, only Rabin had the authority to shake Arafat's hand and give up territory to Palestinian control, and on the Palestinian side only Arafat had the credibility to agree to a Palestinian state on a projected 22 percent of the territory of historic Palestine and no real right of return for the refugees. Oslo was so fragile that one bullet stopped it cold. But just as the cancellation of the Lavi fighter project in the 1980s drove technology back into the civilian market, creating the basis for Israel's high-tech industry, so Oslo left a massive heritage of peace-related thinking, legislation, research, and, most important, an understanding of what peace will ultimately require: an Israel strong enough to make tough decisions and a Palestinian society that has rejected violence and is proud to be with Israel at the touchstone of the new Middle East.

With Israel and the Palestinians at peace, no Arab country will have moral justification for going to war with Israel in the future. Instead of isolation, Israel will enjoy the support of the rational world. With the Israel-Palestinian question out of the way, the Middle East could focus its wealth and energy on development. It would also allow Israel to share the experiences of its own survival, many appropriate and applicable to the region's problems.

Peace with all the Palestinians is not possible now. Gaza, it seems, will remain in the domain of Hamas for a long time to come, and the Palestinians first have to make peace with themselves before Israel can make peace with all of them. The instability in the Arab world in the wake of the Syrian, Tunisian, Egyptian, and Libyan rebellions in early 2011 is worrying and has major strategic consequences for Israel, but it is not a reason for Israel or the Palestinian Authority to be reconsidering peace. If anything, it should provide an impetus: the Palestinian Authority does not want to become engulfed in the same storm that hit the Arab world because of the unfulfilled promises of its leaders. If the West Bank goes up in flames, the Palestinians and Israel both have a lot to lose.

In December 2010 I was privy to hearing how the Israeli defense establishment assessed the situation on the West Bank. It was defined as a "sea change" by an officer who had served in a very senior capacity in the territories who could, technically, be defined as Israel's occupier-in-chief. The strategy of the Palestinian Authority since the June 14, 2007, takeover of Gaza by Hamas, he said, was to root out Hamas on the West Bank, walk away from terror and violence, fight for international recognition for a Palestinian state, de-legitimize Israel's occupation, and come to a settlement that would be honorable and logical, and would give the Palestinians an independent state with Jerusalem as its capital, as well as a face-saving formula for the refugees. The Palestinian Authority removed 1,000 Islamic clergymen associated with Hamas from the mosques in two years, between 2008 and 2010, and 1,500 pro-Hamas teachers were replaced and some returned to the educational system after being "reeducated." All Hamas pirate radio stations were closed down. In tandem the Palestinian Authority continued to build the elements of civil society so that when statehood came, the Palestinians would be accustomed to it. The Canadians worked with the Palestinians on a legal system, training judges and building a court system. The Japanese funded production plants in Jericho. Infrastructure, always Israel's problem, was taken over by the Palestinian Authority: sewage treatment plants, schools, public facilities, and services. With British and American help, the security services went through a total makeover, accepting one out of every seventy applicants. Where armed gangs had ruled, in Jenin and Nablus, for example, parking tickets were now handed out and people fined for crossing the road illegally. But the critical factor was that during 2010, every terrorist attack foiled on the West Bank by Israeli security services was done so with the full cooperation of the Palestinians, this time not as quislings of the Israeli occupation but as the guardians of a civil society in Palestine-to-be.

There are huge risks for Israel in making peace with a Palestinian Authority that is trying to make peace with Hamas. There are also risks in making peace with one part of the Palestinian people and perhaps having to continue to fight the other half, which could only lead to tensions in any peace process. The Palestinians in Gaza are, after all, the brethren of those on the West Bank and Israel is sandwiched between the two. There have been previous disappointments with the Palestinians, and the sorry examples provided by both Gaza and Lebanon that became launching pads for attacks against Israel after being evacuated add caution to danger.

The consequences of failure would be heavy indeed for everyone, but less so for the Palestinians, who may have a fledgling state to lose but who already live under occupation. Israel, however, will have fractured itself internally in the move to vacate settlements and will have spent billions of dollars to do so. It will have removed intelligence and security assets from Palestinian territory, including Palestinian areas that directly overlook sensitive strategic assets, such as Israel's only international airport. It will have given up its military presence on the Jordan River and placed its primary infrastructure and main population centers within missile range of the Palestinians on the West Bank. It would open up the West Bank from the east to arms imports and possible foreign terrorist infiltration and bring threats right up to Israel's border, where the country is narrowest and most densely populated. The collapse of peace would by definition require the reconquest of Palestinian cities on the West Bank by Israel, with all this would entail: Israeli tanks and bulldozers pushing their way through narrow streets of villages chasing terrorists, women and children screaming, the world's television cameras filming away, journalists typing as fast as they can. To accomplish this, Israeli reserves would need to be called up and money diverted from education, health, and infrastructure to war, and Israel's image would take a dive, its officers back on the world's wanted lists, its produce boycotted again in countries like Scandinavia.

Israel would shoulder most of the blame regardless of the reasons for the breakdown of the process, adding another dimension of risk to the significant others: strategic, economic, and diplomatic. If Israel makes peace, agrees to an independent Palestinian state on the West Bank, and withdraws its troops and many of its settlers, and then peace breaks down, it will not be back to square one for Israel, but serious regression on every front. Peace is possible, and developments on the Palestinian side are encouraging, but the risks are tremendous and it is going to take extraordinary leadership on the Israeli side to surmount them, convince the Israeli public that the price of peace is worth the risks, and actually carry through on whatever movement of Israeli population on the West Bank needs to be done. There are interim steps that can be made before full peace, and many in Israel are counseling such an approach, though the Palestinians have had their share of unfulfilled interim agreements and will not settle for another. There is also the escape route of Israeli unilateralism that some may choose to try to delay the day of judgment, when Israel must face the sorry facts of its occupation. At some stage someone in Israeli politics is going to have to bite the bullet if the Palestinians on the West Bank continue to develop into a stable democracy.

Is there such an Israeli leader? The place to find the answer to that question is in the Knesset, where in the wings is a young generation of Israeli politicians whose names may not be familiar even to most Israelis, but who look different, act different, and have a different agenda for their country. The majority are generally moderate in outlook, would prefer peace to war, care about Israeli society and Israel's image abroad, are not xenophobic, want a forward-looking country, respect the law and the High Court, and are deeply democratic. There are fewer generals among them, as was the trend for so long in Israeli politics, where becoming a member of the Knesset seemed almost another rung up on the ladder of rank.

Moshe Dayan, Ariel Sharon, and Yitzhak Rabin were right for their time, but Ehud Barak's performance as prime minister and later as head of the Labor Party contributed a great deal to the public's growing distaste for generals who enter politics and think they can order the electorate around and claim to know what's best for Israel. If it were up to most of the generals, all of Israel would look like Route 443. Until now there has been a very important and encouraging incubation process on the Palestinian side toward a democratic future, and one senses in the corridors of the Knesset that the same consensus toward conciliation is brewing. What has yet to arrive is the leader to make it a reality, but if one looks on the sidelines of the political arena, at the youngsters in their new-looking, ill-fitting, business-like clothes, passing laws that clean up rivers and turn garbage dumps into parks, that ensure a minimum wage and social benefits for the elderly, the country is heading in the right direction.

Among the optimism are shadows in Israeli politics that have to be watched like hawks, such as those who demanded a parliamentary commission of inquiry into the funding of left-wing NGOs and the activities of foreign governments in Israel that supposedly harm Israel, and in particular people like Dr. Michael Ben Ari, a member of the Knesset Law, Justice, and Constitution Committee. One of four members from the extreme right United Nationalist Party (Ichud Haleumi), Ben Ari is an outspoken racist who spews hatred for Arabs and foreign workers, citing biblical injunctions against them and all other goyim in a primitive way that belies the PhD he holds in Israel studies and archaeology. In a sinister political maneuver, he was named chair of the Knesset Subcommittee for the Review of Foreign Donations to Israeli Organizations, which makes a mockery of the subcommittee but leaves Ben Ari and his cohorts convinced that they can bend democracy.

The Israeli Arab factions also have to ensure they don't bend the rules, using the fig leaf of alleged discrimination to justify undemocratic behavior. Some have crossed the line, visiting the enemy during times of war, and making outrageous statements against the state of Israel from the very podium that affords them unique freedom of speech in the Arab world, of which Israel, thankfully, is not part.

One who crossed the line was Azmi Bishara, the leader of the Balad Party, one of the Arab political spinoffs in the Knesset with a purported ideology of creating in Israel "a state for all its citizens," as opposed to Israel being a Jewish state, and for recognition of the Arabs as a national minority. The party's overt agenda and the behavior of its Knesset members, however, were two different things: In 2001 Bishara visited Syria and heaped praise on Hezbollah, and in 2006 he, Wasil Taha, and Jamal Zahalka, all members of the Israeli parliament, visited Damascus in the middle of Israel's war with Hezbollah, praised the Syrians, and went on to Lebanon, where they met with the Lebanese prime minister to tell him that Hezbollah had "lifted the spirit of the Arab people." When the three returned to Israel and were questioned by the security authorities for visiting an enemy country at a time of war, they claimed parliamentary immunity as Knesset members, a claim upheld by the courts. As for Bishara, he fled Israel in April 2007, by the skin of his teeth escaping charges of espionage, money laundering, and treason. He resigned his Knesset membership at the Israeli embassy in Cairo and has not been back since. The charges against him are specific: that he received cash payments in return for information about Israel's strategic targets. A graduate of the Hebrew University in Jerusalem, a full Israeli citizen with free movement of travel, a resident of Nazareth in the middle of the country, a member of the Knesset and some its intimate committees, fluent in Hebrew, and very aware of the public mood in Israel and who was who in politics, he had much to sell Hezbollah.

Bishara's personal behavior and that of his Knesset delegation infuriated the Israeli public and generated a right-wing attempt to get Balad banned in the Knesset as undemocratic and anti-Israel, which failed, again thanks to the High Court, which by a majority of eight to one ruled that Israel's democracy was strong enough to sustain even a voice like Balad's.

Then came Haneen Zoabi, the first woman to appear in the Knesset on behalf of an Arab party, having come in third on Balad's list to the Knesset in the 2009 election. Zoabi, a graduate of Haifa and Jerusalem Universities, came from an old, established Israeli Arab family that counted among its members a former mayor of Nazareth and a deputy minister of health. From the start Zoabi was far more anti-Israel in her rhetoric than the male members of her faction. She called the state "fascist" and praised the Iranian nuclear program, saying it offset Israel's power. Then in May 2010 she boarded the MV *Marmara*, the Turkish ship that was part of a flotilla that tried to break the Gaza blockade. She later produced horrific reports about what happened on the ship when it was boarded by Israeli commandoes and a bloodbath ensued, claiming that the Israeli troops tried to kill as many innocent passengers as they could.

Bishara and Zoabi were not new voices representing the Arab community in the Knesset; they were shriller, more loaded with hatred, and calculated to incite outrage. They are dangerous provocateurs, but few. Bishara and Zoabi do not endanger Israeli democracy itself; they make the position of Israeli Arabs insecure within it. They have read the polls and understand how negative the effect is on the Israeli public's view of Israeli Arabs when members of Balad pose for pictures with Hezbollah's leader in the middle of a war. They hate Israel as a Jewish state and make no bones about it, openly calling for its demise. They are trying to break the system and test the courts and the limits of parliamentary immunity, trying to create situations where Israel will react and be blamed for being antidemocratic, racist, bigoted—all slurs that serve to undermine the state they want to destroy. They don't have a chance. Four Balad members of the Knesset watched closely by the security services are not going to undermine Israel. Neither are any of Israel's Arab politicians if they continue to be dispersed throughout the political system the way they were in 2011 when fourteen Arab and Druze were members of eight rival parties, including the Likud, Labor, Kadima, and even the right-wing Yisrael Beiteinu Party headed by Avigdor Lieberman. The foreign minister in Netanyahu's cabinet, Lieberman was no small threat to democracy himself, wanting to see a system with the justice and finance ministries, the various secret services, and the police under presidential control. He, of course, saw himself as president.

Yet, with all its problems, as has been said, if the rest of the Middle East looked like Israel, it would be a different world, and on the eve of 2011 it began to look as if change were beginning to happen. On December 17, 2010, Mohamed Bouazizi, a Tunisian street vendor who had gotten into a scrap with municipal officials and had his wares confiscated, immolated himself in public. The act was caught on camera and within hours the streets of Tunisia were full of protesters expressing a deep anger against the despotic regime of President Zine el Abidine Ben Ali, Tunisia's autocratic ruler for twenty-three years, who fled for his life with his family (and many billions in public money). With Twitter, Facebook, other Internet applications, and satellite television, particularly Qatar-based Al Jazeera, the heat of Tunisia's "Dignity Revolution" soon caught on. Significantly, in Egypt the population no longer had patience with eighty-two-year-old President Hosni Mubarak, though he was supposed to retire and was known to be on the verge of death with advanced pancreatic cancer. A year earlier the Egyptian president had made the cardinal mistake of naming his son Gamal, or Jimmy, to succeed him and had taken him to Washington on a get-to-know-the-president trip, something that might have washed in Syria, where the population was kept compliant at the edge of a sword, but not in Egypt, where, despite constraints, limited political pluralism and relatively free speech have been the norm. There were more than 20 million registered Internet users in Egypt at the time Bouazizi set himself on fire, and his act, its symbolism, and anger spread like wildfire through the country, years of pent-up frustration over poverty, rising prices, corruption, and the arrogance of the ruling class, all burst out in popular peaceful revolution. Within weeks Mubarak's career as president, which had begun with the assassination of Anwar Sadat in October 1981, ended, as did any hopes of Jimmy succeeding him.

The end of Mubarak's autocratic regime came as no surprise. For years intelligence services around the world had been waiting for him to die. The question was one of the nature of transition, the role of the military and how the fortunes of the Muslim Brotherhood, long suppressed politically, would pan out. It was assumed that in the bad-case scenario (war being the worst case) a new Egyptian government could repudiate the peace treaty with Israel and stop supplying Israel with natural gas. Egyptian gas provides 43 percent of Israel's total needs. The new regime could also close the Suez Canal to Israeli shipping, certainly to Israeli naval vessels en route from the Mediterranean to the Red Sea, and from there to the Gulf, Iran's backyard. The Egyptian military, confined to the western side of the canal by the terms of the peace treaty between the sides, was far from Israeli territory, and Egypt's relatively old air force of five hundred fighters, the most modern of which were sixty-seven early-model F-16s, did not pose a mortal threat to Israel. Where the attitude of the new government would be important was at the crossing points between Egypt and the Gaza Strip, where a relaxation could open new avenues of arms supplies to Hamas, but again this was not seen as a mortal threat to Israel.

Stopping short of war, relations between Israel and Egypt could go from cool to frigid without much of an effect on the overall strategic environment. The Egyptian Muslim Brotherhood was anti-Israel, but it was not anti-West, nor was it at war with the West. It was nonviolent in ideology and believed that Muslim societies should have Muslim values. It was neither Jihadist nor Al-Qaeda in outlook or belief. Also, unlike in some other Middle East countries, the military in Egypt was generally liked. All men in the country, other than the rich, who could buy their way out, were liable for at least one year of military service and nine years of reserve duty, and many of the officers and men sent to control the riots in the 2011 uprisings were relatives of those rioting. Egypt's officers had been trained at U.S. military colleges for over thirty years, and since the Camp David Accords, in which Israel and Egypt made peace, Egypt had received $35 billion in military aid, the largest amount paid out to any country other than Israel.

The stabilizing role played by the military, Egypt's relationship with the United States, the relative moderation of the Muslim Brotherhood in Egypt, the power of the moneyed elite who controlled the economy, and the importance to the world that the Suez Canal remain open all indicated that Egypt could evolve into a Turkey-like state with Islamic overtones, and could very well wind up playing the same role.

The wave of protest that started in Tunis did not end in Egypt, with radical revolts taking place in Libya and Yemen, and the beginning of an uprising in Syria that the regime met with brutal violence. In March 2011 Saudi Arabian forces entered Bahrain to prop up the emirate's beleaguered Sunni king. In Jordan and Morocco kings responded by replacing prime ministers and cabinets with more of the same, and announced pending political reforms. In Yemen the president, Ali Abdullah Saleh, who had ruled since 1978, said that he would step down in 2013, and he, too, eventually sacked his entire cabinet as his spokesmen insisted it was just business as usual, but violent revolution continued and casualties mounted. In the Gulf, royal families rushed to consolidate and began to spread some of their fantastic wealth among the people, hoping for quiet. Libya was plunged into civil war with no one being particularly sure of who the "good guys" were in the fight to dislodge Qaddafi, and NATO seemingly more and more confused about what it was trying to achieve in the country. In Syria, where the minority Alawites ruled, the initial response was to ease up on Internet use in the hope that the demands for democracy reverberating through the Arab world would not land on their doorstep. Bashar Assad, however, was probably tightening the noose around his own neck by doing so. With over four million Internet users in the country of twenty-one million, a literacy rate of over 80 percent, and 40 percent of the country under the age of fourteen, the cork will not stay in the bottle forever. His autocratic regime will have to either give in to change or face the type of increasingly violent rebellion, the first sparks of which were seen in March 2011, when relatively small and peaceful demonstrations for change were met with increasingly violent force.

At the end of the day, all this was healthy for Israel. For the first time in a long time, the Arab world was busy with itself and not obsessing about Israel. The evolution of a stable democracy in Egypt that would be accepted and supported by the people, even with the Muslim Brotherhood in government and at the price of formal peace, is in the long term a better bet than a tyrant with mediocre offspring.

As for Iran, with each passing year its ability to threaten Israel has diminished both due to internal and external factors. The call for democracy resounded with increasing clarity. In a country with almost 85 percent literacy for males and well over 70 percent for women, ten million Internet users, a young population, and a strong underground culture of whiskey, women, and soft drugs, the stern medieval religious mumbo jumbo emanating from the ayatollahs in Qom will not rule forever. In an age where hundreds of Muslim leaders from around the world were going on a pilgrimage to Auschwitz, the regime's Holocaust denial rang as hollow as their threats to wipe Israel off the map. Iran's internal problems are stupendous. The country has double-digit inflation and unemployment, there is a brain drain, and the public sector is inefficient, with services consuming over 40 percent of the country's GDP. The economy is distorted by subsidies and subject to rigid price controls, making it stodgy and difficult to change, and despite being an exporter of crude oil, Iran has virtually no refining capacity, making the country dependent on oil imports for its energy needs. The country is an ethnic mess, with the Sunni terror underground, the Jundallah, becoming ever bolder in its strategically placed suicide-bomber attacks, directed at the regime itself. To top it all, Iran's nuclear program was costing it dearly, not only in terms of cash outlays it could ill afford, but in international sanctions that were beginning to bite and a series of cyber attacks that left its centrifuges spinning in the wrong direction, though production was only slowed, not stopped. The *New York Times* called the STUXNET computer worm that found its way into Iran's nuclear facility in Natanz in late 2010 "the most sophisticated cyber weapon ever deployed." The paper said Israel had built a dummy Iranian nuclear facility in Dimona to test the destructive program, which then mysteriously found its way into the centrifuges used to enrich uranium, supplied to Iran by the German company Siemens, to weapons-grade material.

One consequence of the changes reverberating through the Middle East is that the dividing line between democracy and totalitarianism in the Arab world is that much clearer. Turkey is a democracy; Egypt could be; Saudi Arabia is not. If there is eventually democracy in the Middle East, it will be because Israel has helped plant it. Those Arabs who have come into contact with Israel other than in war have come to value the experience. Even those in areas Israel has occupied recognize some of the values to be adapted from Israeli society, even if only the respect we have for human life and the extent we will go to preserve it.

Can Israel survive? Of course it can. The question is what kind of Israel it will be and what kind of neighbors it might enjoy. How Israel tackles the internal issues of the Hareidim and the Israeli Arabs is important, even critical. But even more important, the nature of Israeli survival depends on whether it remains an occupier or a tyrannical overlord. In continued occupation lies the deepening of internal dissent between the settlers and the rest of Israel, between the Right and Left, those who claim to speak in the name of God and the rest of us. Occupation will lead to the erosion of Israel's moral fiber. Our children serve in the Israeli army, and whatever they learn there, while enforcing the occupation, the roadblocks, and midnight searches, the decision to allow someone through a barrier to visit a sick relative or not, are things they bring home with them.

There is also the impossibility of Israel living forever without an internationally recognized eastern border. Secure, permanent, and recognized boundaries are integral to statehood and independence. There is no such thing as a permanent country with temporary borders.

For Israel democracy is not a choice in terms of a way of life; it is the only mechanism that will ensure that the people of modern Israel can overcome their differences, set national priorities, and do what is necessary to continue to survive in a hostile, volatile, unpredictable, and dangerous part of the world. It allows for civilian control over the military in a country where security is a constant problem, and produces generals who then go into politics and start kissing babies instead of giving orders. Golda

Meir is credited with saying that Israel had as many prime ministers as citizens. Democracy allows them to all express themselves
freely, like the valve on a pressure cooker that allows the steam
to get out. The walls of Israel have never been breached when
the country is united. Democracy fosters unity; occupation undermines it. Liberalism and compassion are as much part of the
Jewish national character as formal religion. Democracy allows
them to live side by side. The settlers are a powerful political force
and the NGOs that watch their every move are a powerful moral
force. Things break down when killings by Israeli settlers of Palestinians in the territories, or abuses of Palestinian property, remain
unresolved, while every Palestinian child who throws a stone soon
finds himself in the uneven wheels of the Israeli military justice
system in the territories. That is why Israel has to stop being an
occupier—not because of Iran or Hezbollah, but because of its
own national soul, that of a Jewish people in their own homeland
who respect others because they can respect themselves.

My biggest consolation in all this is that those who survived
the camps and the Nazis lived to see a proud Jewish state be born
and defend itself. They knew: never again. Their children, who
often had to live their lives with the screams of their parents in
the night, and their grandchildren know they have a Jewish state
they can come to almost no matter their personal circumstances,
even if they have only one grandparent who is Jewish. They will
be looked after with dignity. To have witnessed the absorption
of so many different ethnic groups from so many different countries into this land over the years has been a miracle to behold.
In speaking to the young—those I meet on campuses, the children of our friends and my children, those of my sister and her

children—I find new Israelis with concern for their country who are actively making it better. They live in a society that sees the Internet as a blessing, not a threat, and they can say what they like, how they like, and when they like within the limits of the law. On campuses during a time of emergency, youngsters with tattoos, piercings, and long hair dash between reserve duty and exams. Gavriel and Lev, our two young sons, teens who grew up with suicide bombings and newscasts that were more violent than most video games on the market, have great lives in this country, a good education, excellent health care, involvement in nature and socially oriented youth movements, and not a single doubt about their identity, who they are or their right to be here. They have relatives who are religious and live in the settlements, whom they like and respect but do not identify with ideologically, and other cousins who are pilots and officers in elite units, who are totally secular and have little time for settlers. Like big families anywhere, it takes weddings and funerals to get everyone together, but when they do, they come together as one family, the many different faces of this country, with many opinions, many arguments. But a family.

It is not too late to correct the historical mistake of settled occupation. If it cannot be done with the Palestinians, it has to be done unilaterally, with all the lessons of the painful pullout of the Jewish settlements from Gaza learned, and with as little contention as possible. But the better way to end the occupation is by making peace with the Palestinian Authority on the West Bank in the hope they will eventually be able to deliver the rest of the Palestinian people, and drawing an agreed-upon border between the two sides. Doing so is essential now. I am embarrassed to admit to my politically correct friends in Israel, who do not interact with the territories, that from time to time my Thursday-night poker game takes place in Ma'aleh Adumim, an Israeli city in occupied territory east of Jerusalem that was planned in 1976 and intended as a buffer against a possible invasion from the east—Iraq and Jordan. Now a neat, well-planned, modern, and spotless community of 35,000 and growing, it sits like a bone in the throat of Palestine-to-be. Every time we travel there, through a series of tunnels that run under Mount Scopus and on a super-modern highway, I am amazed at how the place seems to be growing, like an octopus spreading its tentacles over the biblical hills of the Judean desert that flow down toward the Dead Sea. Each time there seem to be more lights, another shopping mall, more development carried out in the shadows of a stagnated peace process, inept administrations in Washington, weak Israeli leadership, and tired Palestinian leaders who have to carry the dual burden of providing for a country while not having one. As an Israeli I feel that I have lost before I even get to the game, given the massive resources being spent on this anachronism in the desert, this impediment to normalcy in any future peace process. And then gamble our evening away.

That has to end. Israel cannot waste its resources. It cannot be unfocused. It cannot gamble for its future. Money put into Ma'aleh Adumim is good money after bad. Iran, with all its problems, Hezbollah, Hamas, the Muslim Brotherhood, Al-Qaeda, the Islamic Jihad, English anti-Israel academics, unions in Norway—all wish Israel away. Investing one more cent in Ma'aleh Adumim, or any other settlement at this time, is like dealing them the hand to achieve their goal. Settlements waste resources,

249

they complicate any prospect of peace, they compromise Israel as a democracy, and they give ammunition to Israel's enemies. They have created a young settler generation, some of whom have no respect for the law, and have spawned yet more illegal settlements all over the territories. Their conduct can no longer be tolerated. With or without peace, Israel cannot have citizens living with two different codes of law. If I were to draw a gun and shoot a Palestinian throwing a stone on my street in Jerusalem, I would be locked up for a long time. If I did so in Kiryat Arba or Jewish Hebron, I would be a hero. The dichotomy is morally debilitating and destructive.

Looking at Israel is a bit like going to an impressionist exhibition. If you stand close up and read the headlines each day, all you see are the individual incidents—the daubs of paint. It takes some distance to see the picture, or at least to gain some clarity. It takes someone to ask the question as to whether Israel can survive to grapple with the answer and realize the question is more whether Iran and Syria, Egypt and Tunisia, Lebanon and Yemen, and Iraq will survive, and if so, what they will look like. Some of these giants have to deal with populations of eighty million and growing at a time of diminishing resources. In Israel's case, its defense expenditure has gone down since the mid-1970s, when it was 34 percent of GNP, to just over 7–9 percent today, despite the Iranian and other threats the country faces. Egypt could cut off its gas but Israel's recent finds at the Tamar and Leviathan fields off its northern Mediterranean coast can supply the country's needs for decades. Water has always been central to Israel's strategic thinking, and that of its enemies. In 2011 the cornerstone was laid for a privately owned and operated desalination plant near Ashkelon that alone will provide half of what Israel used to siphon off the Kinneret. New tax proceeds to the state from these enterprises would more than compensate if, for whatever reason, the American administration decided to cut its aid to Israel.

I don't believe I am living in a fool's paradise but the figures speak for themselves: 97 percent of men and 96 percent of women in Israel are literate; the median age in the country is a responsible and respectable twenty-nine, life expectancy is around eighty years, and 4.5 million Israelis use the Internet. The emigration rate is only 2.2 per 1,000; it has the most highly developed telephone and public transportation systems in the Middle East; and in 2009, there were 9.22 million cell phones for 7.5 million people.

On the map and from a helicopter this is a small and fragile country. The looming skylines of Tel Aviv and the surrounding cities grow impressively against the Mediterranean but are reminders of how densely populated and vulnerable the center is. The Iranians, the Syrians, Hezbollah, and Hamas, all armed with missiles with the accuracy and the range to wreak havoc among the skyscrapers of Israel's cities, are not going to make peace with Israel in a hurry, even if there is dramatic internal change. Business and quiet normalization, however, are another thing if and only if the Palestinian issue is off the table. Israel has been offered a formal peace treaty with the Arab world in the form of the Arab Peace Initiative, adopted by the Arab League in Beirut in 2002 and re-endorsed at the Riyadh Summit in 2007. The youngsters waiting in the Knesset for their turn at the helm should retrieve and read it.

They should also work out what type of education we could be giving the country's children and the level of care that could be afforded to the elderly generation that built this country, if significant resources were not wasted on building where Israel has no future.

Though they are young, those waiting in the wings have fought their wars, and they know what the country needs for its future. They have parents and grandparents here, not memories of ghosts from the ghetto. Modern Israel is a new seed planted in an ancient land. It has struggled to fruition, but it has taken root and today stands firm. Now, not merely to survive but to thrive, its roots have to take hold in its own soil, so that it can grow to provide shade and solace, beauty and strength, and all that God intended. Amen.

* * *

My son Gavriel will be conscripted into the Israeli army in a few years. Already he is running and doing pushups, keeping his weight in line, and thinking about which unit to serve in and privately, I'm sure, whether he wants to be a soldier at all. His brother Shai and sister, Maya, have been there before him, and his little brother, Lev, may yet have to go if Israel still needs an army by then, something we continue to hope will not be the case but do not expect.

I know no purer soul than Gavriel. There is not an ounce of bad in his taut little body. He has strong values, a deep understanding of the world around him, a love for Israel and his fellow man. He is a youth leader, a good student, a lover of nature and animals. He also loves to travel, see, and explore, and to read. He is ever curious. I rely on Gavriel as much as I would on any person, trust his judgment, and am in awe of his honesty and integrity. He is a boy who, because of the closeness of the intifada to home, fears Arabs but wants peace; is dubious of the details but understands it has to be done. He is fair, knows how to apologize, and has a deep social awareness. I say all this not in self-congratulation, but because there are many like Gavriel in Israeli society. I see them all the time. Gavriel is a product of modern Israeli society, of its school system, youth movement, culture, and synagogue. I look deeply into the black pools of his eyes and see Israel's future, deep and full of light. I love and respect him and am proud he is a sabra. May he serve his people well, and may his people serve him well. Hopefully they deserve each other.

ACKNOWLEDGMENTS

This book is to a large degree a product of osmosis, absorbing knowledge and insights from my colleagues at the Institute for National Security Studies at Tel Aviv University. Over the decade we have worked together, I have benefited from their experience and wisdom, and gained respect for the painstaking research that is at the heart of the institute. I am also deeply thankful for the luxury of time the institute afforded me in writing this book.

I would like to express my gratitude to my friend and agent, Michael Levine, who waited patiently for this book, as did Clive Priddle, my editor at PublicAffairs, who has done so much to improve this manuscript.

Both Michael and Clive at times seemed to have more faith in me than I had in myself while wrestling with the masses of material that needed to be ingested and structured to make coherent sense of the subject. If I have failed to do so, however, the fault is entirely mine.

ACKNOWLEDGMENTS

I would like to also thank Jeremy, Levi, Roberta, Elise, and Calev, who all helped me greatly—each in their own way. I have decided not to include notes and a bibliography. In this day and age of multiple search engines, those who have a desire to get deeper information on any given point can do so in a matter of seconds, just as I did. I cannot express what an incredible tool the Internet is, and in that context I want to thank the anonymous authors and editors of resources such as the CIA *World Factbook*, which I used throughout the book.

And above all I would like to thank Isabel Kershner Goodman, whose advice and love along the way has been immense, invaluable, and deeply appreciated.

Hirsh Goodman
Jerusalem
March 2011

INDEX

INDEX

Riki Rosen

HIRSH GOODMAN is a senior research associate at the Institute for National Security Studies at Tel Aviv University, where he directs the Bronfman Program on Information Strategy. Prior to joining INSS in August 2000, Goodman was vice president of the *Jerusalem Post*. In 1990 he founded the *Jerusalem Report* and served as its editor-in-chief for eight years. Between 1986 and 1989 he was the strategic fellow at the Washington Institute for Near East Policy, where he authored, with W. Seth Carus, *The Future Battlefield and the Arab-Israel Conflict*. He has also written an official history of the Israeli navy and many documentary films. His memoir, *Let Me Create a Paradise, God Said to Himself*, was published by PublicAffairs, New York, and HarperColllins, Canada, in 2005. Goodman was born in Port Elizabeth, South Africa, in March 1946 and immigrated to Israel in February 1965. He lives in Jerusalem.

PublicAffairs is a publishing house founded in 1997. It is a tribute to the standards, values, and flair of three persons who have served as mentors to countless reporters, writers, editors, and book people of all kinds, including me.

I. F. STONE, proprietor of *I. F. Stone's Weekly*, combined a commitment to the First Amendment with entrepreneurial zeal and reporting skill and became one of the great independent journalists in American history. At the age of eighty, Izzy published *The Trial of Socrates*, which was a national bestseller. He wrote the book after he taught himself ancient Greek.

BENJAMIN C. BRADLEE was for nearly thirty years the charismatic editorial leader of *The Washington Post*. It was Ben who gave the *Post* the range and courage to pursue such historic issues as Watergate. He supported his reporters with a tenacity that made them fearless and it is no accident that so many became authors of influential, best-selling books.

ROBERT L. BERNSTEIN, the chief executive of Random House for more than a quarter century, guided one of the nation's premier publishing houses. Bob was personally responsible for many books of political dissent and argument that challenged tyranny around the globe. He is also the founder and longtime chair of Human Rights Watch, one of the most respected human rights organizations in the world.

•   •   •

For fifty years, the banner of Public Affairs Press was carried by its owner Morris B. Schnapper, who published Gandhi, Nasser, Toynbee, Truman, and about 1,500 other authors. In 1983, Schnapper was described by *The Washington Post* as "a redoubtable gadfly." His legacy will endure in the books to come.

Peter Osnos, *Founder and Editor-at-Large*